D0948304

Italian cooking

ROBIN HOWE

Foreword by **Jennifer Paterson**

ANDRE DEUTSCH

First published in Great Britain in 1953 by André Deutsch Ltd

This edition first published in 1998 by André Deutsch Ltd
76 Dean Street
London W1V 5HA

www.vci.co.uk

André Deutsch is a VCI plc company

1 3 5 7 9 10 8 6 4 2

Printed and bound in Great Britain by St Edmundsbury Press, Suffolk

A catalogue record for this book is available from the British Library

ISBN 0 233 99473 4

Design by Kee Scott Associates

Contents

Italian cooking

Foreword

Robin Howe's *Italian Cooking* flows with her usual exhilaration and charm. It is a thoroughly comprehensive book of Italian food with all the pasta, rice and polenta variations, differing forms of gnocchi, meat, lots of wonderful fish and sea food, vegetables and very good, unusual salads.

However, it was written a long time ago, when Britain was not awash with Italian restaurants and delicatessens. So, when Robin gives long grain rice for risottos and soups we must now replace this with arborio, roma or carnaroli, which are the superfino rices that take longer to cook, and absorb a lot of liquid during cooking without breaking up. Also she uses cottage cheese instead of ricotta which is no longer necessary. Don't buy supermarket ricotta, always go for the freshly made variety to be found in the delicatessens. Two other points to be noted: the *Melanzane alla Romana* should be made with mozzarella not ricotta or cottage cheese, and the delicious gremolata, which is sprinkled over *Osso Buco*, should have a good tablespoon of grated lemon rind added to the parsley and garlic.

Within these pages there are quantities of great Italian dishes which vary so enormously from region to region and, dear to my heart, special feast day foods for different saints days and religious festivals. I am still trying to hunt down the feast of the Impruneta when *Pollo alla Diavola* is devoured.

There is a good chapter of very rich puddings which the Italians adore, though these are never mentioned when the diet high-priests recommend the Mediterranean way of eating.

Enjoy it all.

Jennifer Paterson

Introduction

Italian cooking is Mediterranean cooking and for many people Mediterranean cooking at its best. It is not complicated, much of it is distinctly earthy, so it allows itself to be reproduced in many parts of the world.

Those who judge Italian cooking carelessly claim that it is all spaghetti, garlic, olive oil and tomatoes, a claim which considerably annoys the Italians and is not even half true. Those foreigners who go to Italy without doing some culinary homework can be persuaded that Italian cooking is all spaghetti or noodles, but this is because so many of them, unable to speak Italian, are baffled by the menu and are far too shy to ask the waiter, so that they end by settling for familiar spaghetti and tomato sauce. And remember that, although it is possible to get any amount of pasta dishes throughout Italy, in the north rice is generally preferred.

There are two distinct cooking cultures in this country of extremely individual cooking: one, the wine and olive school, and, two, the milk and butter school. It is simply a matter of what grows where. Garlic is favoured in most regions but it is seldom used excessively; in Tuscany onions are used far more than garlic. Tomatoes reign supreme in southern Italy, but it is difficult to conceive of any Italian cooking without a tomato lurking in some corner or other.

Buy Italian pasta whenever you can. This is not propaganda but common sense. Pasta is an Italian product. In Italy a great many small shops make fresh pasta of all kinds daily, which is quite delicious. In Britain, fresh pasta is now freely available.

Meat, generally speaking, is expensive in Italy and in some parts of the country not all that good. As a result, much of the meat is boiled or cut into small pieces, both for easier cooking and also to tenderize the meat; or it is left to simmer for hours in a mixture of vegetables, often tomatoes, or in red wine until it falls from the bone. Chicken, poultry and game also appear in many guises and in some areas roast pig on a spit is sold in the markets and public squares.

Fish is important, naturally, in a country where so many people live within a few miles of the sea, with plenty of exotic kinds as well as fish of a more everyday British nature. Many different types of fish are available in Britain, but even when the original fish is not available, an Italian dish is still possible. Sprats or smelts can be used instead of sardines, for example; and halibut for tuna or swordfish.

An important feature of Italian cooking is the use of sauces, which are served with meat, fish and vegetables, as well as the numerous pasta dishes.

Italian cooking

Cheese also appears in numerous recipes but is always used with care for, as the Italians say, too much 'will spoil the touch of the food on the tongue'.

Another important ingredient in Italian cooking is wine, often added with a lavish hand. There are the everyday local wines, good for drinking and cooking, and which are cheap in Italy.

Although the Italians have a vast repertoire of sweet dishes, mouth-watering cakes and pastries, they are seldom served to finish a meal; instead they eat fruit, always fruit in season, and what they are pleased to call *macedoine*, in other words, chopped fruit laced with local wines or liqueurs. Another favourite is pears served with cheese, in particular Parmesan, which, when eaten fresh, is one of the finest cheeses in the world. For cooking it is matured until hard enough to grate.

The order of an Italian meal is somewhat similar to our own, except that the Italian likes to start with an antipasto, which can be anything: for instance, a paper-thin slice of prosciutto, or smoked ham, served alone or wrapped round a wedge of sweet melon or with fresh figs, a dish of cooked vegetables, or a plate of spaghetti. In other words, Italians do not start their meal with the main course and they most certainly do not consider that a dish of spaghetti or other pasta constitutes a meal.

Soups are popular and varied, and these come both hot and cold, thick and thin. Some, like *risi e bisi*, are so thick they are eaten with a fork. Italian fish soups (*brodetto*) are served all round the long coastline and each fishing port claims to make the best.

After the antipasto comes the main course, usually served with a salad, almost never with cooked vegetables, since these are considered a dish in their own right.

On the whole Italians do not drink hard liquor. They have their wines, aperitifs and liqueurs; usually they drink wine with their meals but few Italians will drink wine on an empty stomach.

Most of the ingredients used in Italian cooking are now freely available. Even so, a little advice might be of use.

Olive oil has a distinctive taste and differs not only from country to country but also from region to region. Therefore, when preparing Italian dishes do try to find Italian olive oil. Not because it is any better but simply for its particular flavour. Also I prefer to use Italian tinned tomatoes for Italian dishes. This also applies to tomato purée.

Italian salami or mortadella are sausages which are generally available, but prosciutto or finely sliced Italian ham is not. This is very expensive even in Italy. However, a good substitute for it could be some paper-thin slices of smoked bacon.

Olives and anchovies are usually available loose in delicatessen stores or Italian shops, and are cheaper and rather stronger in taste than those in jars. All butter should be unsalted. Italian wines have their own particular aroma and taste, and are widely available.

It is probably easier to become an 'expert' in Italian cooking than it is in any other kind, and it is certainly almost impossible to avoid becoming an enthusiast.

Robin Howe

Seasoning, Herbs and Spices

In this list only those spices and herbs have been given which are more generally used in Italy and which are available in Britain. Whenever possible it is obviously better to use fresh herbs. If you are not used to herbs and spices in cooking, start by being overcautious; they should add a subtle flavour to a dish, and not drown other tastes. After a time you will discover that herbs rightly used become something personal in your cooking and that most dishes, even tried favourites, gain something with the addition of herbs.

Star Anise

Anise
This is often put into cakes, pastries and cottage cheese dishes.

Basil

Basilico
One of the most popular herbs in Italian cooking. Use it fresh in salads, ragouts, stews, savoury dishes, sauces and soups, bisques. Strongly flavoured, the sweet variety is most favoured. Can be used dried.

Bay Leaf

Lauro
One leaf is usually enough to flavour a dish. Use in sauces, soups, stews and most fish dishes.

Borage

Borraggine
Use the young leaves in salads. Italians make fritters with the firmer, larger borage leaves.

Italian cooking

Capers

Capperi
Extensively used in Italian cooking, especially with fish and vegetables.

Chilli Peppers

Pepe Forte
Small red peppers. Use with moderation when a hot pungent flavour is needed.

Cinnamon

Cannella
Use the sticks whenever possible; the flavour is better and they can be used several times.

Cloves

Chiodi di Garofono
Use both whole and ground, especially when flavouring meat and game dishes. Excellent in soups.

Fennel

Finocchio
Greatly favoured by the Italians, who grow the thick variety, which looks a little like celery. Used in salads, and cooking generally.

Garlic

Aglio
Use freely but wisely in almost all savoury and vegetable dishes.

Mace

Scorza di Noce Moscato
Use in savoury dishes as well as sweet.

Marjoram

Maggiorana
Very popular in Italy where the sweet variety is preferred.

Mint

Menta
Use in omelettes, stews and savoury dishes, also in salads but less often in sauce.

Nutmeg

Noce Moscato
Use in meat and savoury dishes as well as in cakes, etc.

Oregano

Origano
A variety of marjoram which is used in the same way.

Paprika

Paprika
Use as a flavouring and as a garnish. Generally the sweet Hungarian variety is preferred. This is not hot, but has a pleasant almost sweet flavour.

Italian cooking

Pine Nuts

Pinoli
Very small white bullet-shaped nuts or kernels. Excellent with rice and other savoury dishes, typically Mediterranean.

Pistachio

Pistacchio
Bright green nuts, used in cakes, sweets and ice-creams.

Parsley

Prezzemolo
Use in almost every savoury dish, especially when garlic has been included.

Rosemary

Rosmarino
Use with poultry, fish and veal. Its somewhat bitter taste changes during cooking to a more delicate flavour.

Saffron

Zafferano
A dull orange coloured spice. Use it for its flavour and its colour. Particularly good in savoury rice dishes. It is expensive but one only needs it in tiny quantities.

Sage

Salvia
The Italians love this herb and use it all the time.

Tarragon

Dragoncella
Use fresh, both for its flavour and decorative appearance. Excellent in soups, sauces, ragouts, etc.

Thyme

Timo
Use plentifully in all types of savoury dishes.

Vanilla

Vaniglia
Use the pods, as their flavour is better than any essence. They can be used again and again.

Italian cooking

Hors d'Oeuvre
Antipasto

Italian antipasto is as regional as all Italian cooking and varies tremendously from the elegant and rather more formal approach of the Bolognese to the simple vegetables, olives, sweet peppers, etc., of the Sicilian.

Although antipasto is an integral part of the Italian cuisine, many people dispense with this course nowadays and start with either a rice or a spaghetti dish, depending on whether they are from the North or South.

The recipes and suggestions given in this chapter are those more generally served, to the accompaniment of a typical mild Italian aperitif.

Fish

Filleted anchovies; sardines fried and stuffed; oysters served *au naturel* or on strips of bread previously spread with caviar; tinned tuna fish with slices of sweet peppers; any of the fish *fritto misto*; shrimps and prawns served either very simply with lemon juice or with salad cream.

Eggs

Hard-boiled and sliced, garnished with anchovies or mayonnaise; devilled and baked, stuffed with various piquant mixtures.

Ham

Usually tangy flavoured prosciutto is used, always paper-thin sliced and served with green and purple figs, or spread with honey. In the melon season it is served with thin slices of ice-cold green melon.

Meats

Here the Italians excel and a plate of cold meats, all beautifully sliced and garnished with aspic, is a joy. It will include cold beef, cooked very rare; lamb and ham; pork and veal; sliced meat galantine; all kinds of piquant sausages, salami and the like; mortadella flavoured with pistachio nuts; in fact, almost every type of meat or sausage one is likely to meet.

Italian cooking

Melon

In season this is very popular, served either with prosciutto, or quite plain flavoured with sugar, or well-soaked in wine. This is done by cutting off a small round at the top of the melon, scooping out all the seeds, and pouring in a glass of Marsala or sherry. It is then almost frozen and served in small cubes.

Sundries

Other suggestions are pickled mushrooms and onions, olives both green and black, cubes of tuna fish with red peppers, tomatoes raw and cooked, slivers of white cheese, tartlets with savoury fillings and garnished with anchovies or mayonnaise; small and large pizza, canapés smeared with mullet roe, smoked salmon, and home-made pastes, croquettes of spinach or meat, or of potato well-flavoured with cheese.

Cheese and Black Olives Fried Together

Formaggio con Olive Nere

Cut 100g (4oz) of mozzarella cheese into cubes and stone 12 ripe black olives. Fry them together in butter until the cheese is blistered and amber coloured. Add a tablespoon of dry white wine, bring to the boil and simmer for 2 minutes. Spread on buttered toast and sprinkle with black pepper.

Fried Cheese Slices

Chizze con Formaggio

150g (5oz) plain flour
25g (1oz) butter
100g (4oz) grated fresh
  Parmesan cheese

1 egg
Pinch salt
Olive oil for frying

Sift the flour and salt together then rub in the butter. Mix with the egg and a little cold water to make a pastry. Leave for 1 hour. Roll out the pastry very thin, sprinkle generously with grated cheese, then pat the cheese into it. Cut the pastry into squares and fry in deep boiling fat until crisp and amber colour.

Parmesan Cheese Bread Fingers

Crostini alla Parmigiana

Cut several slices of stale white bread into fingers. Soak these for 15 minutes in milk. Sprinkle with salt and pepper and thoroughly coat with grated fresh Parmesan cheese. Pat the cheese well into the bread with the back of a wooden spoon, and fry the fingers in hot oil or butter until brown and crisp.

Green Olives, Sicilian Style

Olive Verdi alla Siciliana

Green olives immersed in cold water, salted and flavoured with fennel to taste. They should be left for several days.

Italian cooking

Fried Marrow, Milanese Style

Zucchini alla Milanese

3 courgettes
1–2 beaten eggs
Olive oil for frying

Breadcrumbs
Salt and pepper

Wash the courgettes and cook them in boiling, salted water for 15 minutes. Drain and cut them into 6mm (1/4in) thick slices. Cut off the skin. Dip the slices in beaten egg and coat with seasoned breadcrumbs. Fry in very hot oil until brown on both sides. Reduce the heat and simmer gently for 5 minutes.

Stuffed Cucumbers

Cetrioli alla Duse

2 cucumbers
8 anchovies
2 eggs
1 tablespoon vinegar
English mustard powder

1 small onion
2–3 radishes
Olive oil
Tomato and lemon for
  garnishing

Wash the cucumbers and cut off their ends. Slice them into lengths about 3.5cm (1/2in) long. Put them into boiling water, add the vinegar and cook them for just 5 minutes.

Boil the eggs until hard, chop and mash them until smooth. Mix with a teaspoon of mustard, the onion, very finely chopped, the anchovy, well-chopped, and the radishes, previously grated. Add enough olive oil to bind these ingredients. Scoop out the centres of the cucumber 'tubes', mix the centres with the egg mixture, and refill the cucumber pieces with it. Serve cold, surrounded by slices of raw tomato and wedges of lemon.

Marinated Courgettes

Zucchini in Salmi

450g (1lb) courgettes
Wine vinegar
Bay leaves, clove and pepper
1 sliced onion

1 sliced carrot
Salt and pepper
Olive oil for frying

Wash and slice the courgettes. Fry in hot oil until brown on both sides. Cover and simmer for 5 minutes. Drain and put into a flat dish.

Bring equal quantities of vinegar and water to the boil, enough to cover the slices of courgette, and add the remaining ingredients. Allow to cool then pour this marinade over the courgettes. Leave for 24 hours.

Devilled Eggs

Uova Ripiene

6 hard-boiled eggs
Salt and pepper
Onion juice to taste
Olive oil
150ml (1/4 pint) béchamel sauce

Capers
Anchovies
Gherkin
Chopped fresh parsley

Cut the eggs into halves crossways, then cut off the tips so that they will stand upright. Scoop out the yolks and mix with salt, pepper, a very little olive oil and onion juice. Mash until smooth, then pile back into the whites. Garnish each egg with capers, anchovies and gherkin. Arrange in a shallow casserole and bake at 150°/300°F/Gas 2 for 5 minutes. Put on to a hot dish, cover with hot béchamel sauce, sprinkle with chopped fresh parsley and serve hot.

Italian cooking

Stuffed Peppers

Peperoni Ripieni

6 large green peppers
100g (4oz) white breadcrumbs
Handful fresh parsley, chopped
1 clove garlic, chopped

6 chopped tomatoes
12 anchovies
100g (4oz) cooked long-grain rice
125ml (4fl oz) oil

Wash the peppers, neatly cut off the tops and scoop out the core and seeds. Drop in boiling water and cook for exactly 3 minutes.

Heat the oil and fry the garlic and breadcrumbs, add the tomatoes and simmer until these are soft. Add remaining ingredients and stir well. Fill the peppers with this mixture. Replace the tops of the peppers.

Put the peppers in a baking pan, cover the bottom with boiling water and bake at 190°C/375°F/Gas 5 for 15 to 20 minutes, or until the peppers are soft.

Remove the tops before serving and serve with tomato sauce (see pages 216–7).

Spinach Dumplings

Poepettine di Spinaci

450g (1lb) cooked spinach
225g (8oz) cottage cheese
50g (2oz) grated fresh
  Parmesan cheese
2 egg yolks
25g (1oz) plain flour

75g (3oz) butter
Salt and pepper
Pinch nutmeg
1 teaspoon sugar
1 tablespoon single cream

Melt the butter, add the flour and cook to a roux. Add the cream (taking great care that the pan is not too hot) and then the spinach. Stir well, remove from the heat and add the cottage cheese, Parmesan, seasonings, sugar and nutmeg. Blend well and bind with well-beaten yolks. The mixture must be firm enough to roll into dumplings.

Have ready a large pan with boiling salted water. Roll the spinach mixture into dumplings the size of a walnut and drop them, one by one, into the boiling water. Poach them for 5 minutes, then take them out with a perforated spoon. Serve hot, generously sprinkled with grated Parmesan cheese and with a tomato sauce (pages 216–7).

These dumplings are equally good fried in hot butter or oil instead of being poached, and shaped as croquettes.

Italian cooking

Stuffed Baked Tomatoes

Pomidoro Ripieni alla Casalinga

8 large tomatoes
175g (6oz) cooked minced beef
  or lamb
1–2 beaten eggs
25g (1oz) dried mushrooms
75g (3oz) grated fresh
  Parmesan cheese
50g (2oz) soft breadcrumbs

Handful chopped fresh parsley
Salt and pepper
1 onion, chopped
1 carrot, chopped
1 stick celery, chopped
1 teaspoon sugar
1 clove garlic, chopped
125ml (4fl oz) olive oil

Soak the mushrooms for 20 minutes, then wash well and chop finely. Wash the tomatoes, cut off the tops and scoop out the insides.

Heat the oil, fry the chopped vegetables, garlic, parsley, meat and mushrooms. Add salt, pepper and sugar, then simmer until the vegetables are soft. Remove from the heat, cool slightly, then add the beaten egg(s), breadcrumbs and cheese. Pile this mixture lightly into the tomato cases, sprinkle with a little more cheese and breadcrumbs and cover with the tomato tops. Place in a large baking tin, pour in boiling water and bake at 190°C/375°F/Gas 5 for 30 minutes.

Florentine Toast

Crostini alla Fiorentina

Toast or fry as many slices of bread as required. Keep hot. Sauté in butter 1 small grated onion, some sliced chicken livers and a handful of chopped parsley. Add 2 anchovies and 150ml (¼ pint) of dry white wine. Thicken the sauce with cream or flour, sprinkle with salt, pepper and paprika. Cover the slices of toast with the chicken livers and sauce.

Rice 'Telephone' Croquettes

Suppli dì Riso

A popular Roman antipasto. It is a type of rice croquette filled with meat, onion, etc., and diced mozzarella cheese. When the croquettes are eaten the cheese forms long strings or telephone wires.

450g (1lb) long-grain rice
75g (3oz) grated fresh
  Parmesan cheese
1 tablespoon mushrooms,
  chopped
1 onion, chopped
2 rashers cooked streaky
  bacon, chopped
50g (2oz) cooked minced
  beef or lamb

50g (2oz) butter
Salt and pepper
Stock or water
3 beaten eggs
Diced mozzarella
Breadcrumbs and
  plain flour
Oil

Cook the rice in plenty of boiling stock or water for 10 to 15 minutes. Drain and mix with half the Parmesan cheese and 1 well-beaten egg. Leave to cool and prepare the filling.

Melt the butter and fry the onion, bacon, mushrooms and, lastly, the meat. Mix to a paste, remove from the heat and add the second beaten egg and the rest of the Parmesan cheese.

Take 1 tablespoon of rice, put it in the palm of your hand and smooth it out with the back of a wooden spoon. Place a portion of the filling in the centre with a piece of diced mozzarella. Close your hand in such a way that the rice completely envelops the filling. Shape into croquettes, roll in flour, the third beaten egg and breadcrumbs. Fry in deep boiling oil until a golden brown and serve hot.

Italian cooking

Spaghetti, Rice and Noodles
Pasta e Riso

Spaghetti, Rice and Noodles
Pasta e Riso

While the South loves its pasta dishes the North prefers rice, and some northern Italians will tell you with the utmost scorn that pasta is not to be found in the North at all. This is not entirely true, but it is a fact that all the best rice dishes come from the North and almost every northern Italian would rather eat rice than spaghetti. So while the South is busy preparing its numerous pastas the North is turning out one risotto after another, and while these are not quite so various as the rival pastas, it would be possible to produce a slim volume of recipes for them and their accompanying sauces and garnishes.

Gnocchi and polenta are not loves of my own, but they are generally popular with Italians, and the man from Rome is immensely proud of his version of potato gnocchi, while the man from Milan boasts of his prowess with polenta (cornmeal). It would be possible to write a whole chapter on them, but I think that my Italian friends will agree that many of these doubtless famous recipes are variations on a theme.

Pasta is another matter, for Italy has an incredible number of pasta products. It is said that their names run into thousands, but the number of the different varieties is more likely to be about one hundred and fifty. Identical products carry different names in different regions, and this makes it rather puzzling for the foreign gourmet intent on trying different forms of pasta.

Concerning the origin of pasta there are several legends. The Neapolitans declare that the name macaroni came from a Cardinal of their town who on being presented with it for the first time exclaimed in joy 'Ma caroni' (the little dears). Another legend says that noodles, etc. came from China via an Italian sailor who had learnt the art of making and preparing them from a Chinese lady. Marco Polo, too, is credited with having brought a load of noodles back with him from his long travels, with other rather more valuable cargo.

Whatever their origin, there is seemingly no end to their shapes and sizes. Today even the most diligent Italian cook will buy manufactured spaghetti, vermicelli, and even the minute *anolini* so popular in soups. A good cook, however, still makes ravioli at home, also the *manicotti*, little stuffed hats, sometimes called cima, and usually lasagne (wide noodles) and tagliatelle (noodle or ravioli pastry) for special occasions.

Fillings and sauces for all these pastas are also legion. Most of them contain tomato, but there are exceptions even to this rule. Each district has its speciality, in fact the Italians go one better than this and have special

Italian cooking

sauces or fillings for Festivals and Holy Days, and these can be very rich indeed. Cheese is almost (but not quite) always served with pasta dishes.

For 4 people use 450g (1lb) of pasta or of rice.

Noodle Pastry

Tagliarini

Sieve 900g (2lb) of strong plain flour with a good pinch of salt on to a pastry board. Make a hollow in the centre and break 8 eggs into it. Add the cream. Using a wooden fork, stir the flour into the eggs until a perfectly smooth mass is formed. Knead this as you would bread. Leave to stand for 30 minutes before using.

Noodles. Take the ball of dough and divide it into 6 pieces. Shape each piece into a ball and roll out to almost paper-thin rounds of equal size. Roll each round, as if making a Swiss roll, and cut them into strips, using a very sharp knife. The width of the strips depends on their later use, narrow for soup, medium for general use, or wide when making a dish of lasagne. But the width is really a matter of taste. The strips can be used at once or left to dry for a while.

To make green noodle pastry, add just enough cooked and sieved spinach to give the pastry a pale green shade, and omit the cream. Allow to dry for 10 minutes longer. It is worth the trouble of making flat noodles and noodle pastry at home as the flavour is so much better than the commercially produced noodles. It also takes only a matter of up to 5 minutes to boil fresh pasta until tender or al dente.

Buttered Noodles

Fettuccine all' Alfredo

450g (1lb) noodles   Butter
Grated fresh Parmesan cheese

Cook the noodles in rapidly boiling salted water for 8 to 10 minutes. Drain and mix with plenty of fresh butter, which should not be melted beforehand. Serve with grated Parmesan cheese.

Baked Green Noodles with Cheese

Lasagne Verdi al Forno

450g (1lb) wide green noodles   2 tablespoons olive oil
300ml (1/2 pint) béchamel sauce   Grated fresh Parmesan cheese
1 onion, chopped   50g (2oz) tomato purée
1 carrot, chopped   150ml (1/4 pint) dry white wine
1 stick celery, chopped   150ml (1/4 pint) chicken or
Salt and pepper   vegetable stock
100g (4oz) cooked minced
  beef or lamb

Heat the oil, brown the onion, carrot and celery, then the meal. Dilute the tomato purée with the stock, add this to the meat and vegetables and simmer for 15 minutes. Add the wine, salt and pepper and continue to cook until the vegetables are very soft.

Cook the noodles in rapidly boiling salted water for 8 minutes. Drain and pat them dry, separating the strips. Well-grease an oven casserole and cover the bottom with a layer of noodles. Spread this with meat and vegetables and with the béchamel sauce and sprinkle with grated Parmesan cheese. Cover with another layer of noodles and repeat these layers until all the ingredients are used up, ending with Parmesan.

Cook at 230°C/450°F/Gas 8 until the cheese has browned.

Noodles and Potato with Garlic Sauce

Trenette col Pesto alla Genovese

Boil 225g (8oz) of potatoes in their skins until soft. Drain, peel and slice thickly into rounds. Cook 225g (8oz) of noodles for 8 minutes in rapidly boiling salted water. Drain and mix with the sliced potatoes. Pour over them some thinned pesto (page 62) and sprinkle liberally with grated fresh Parmesan cheese. Serve immediately. This is a Genoese speciality.

Stuffed Macaroni Cannelloni

Maccheroni Ripieni alla Toscana

The macaroni used in this recipe is short and thick, and looks like sawn-up lengths of drainpipe. Cook it for 10 minutes in rapidly boiling water and drain it carefully so that the pieces keep their shape. Allow it to cool sufficiently to handle.

Have ready a typical Italian meat stuffing (page 98, for example). Push this filling into the macaroni tubes and arrange carefully in a large pan. Add stock to cover and cook for another 5 minutes. Serve with a tomato sauce and grated fresh Parmesan cheese.

Macaroni Timbale

Timballo di Maccheroni

225g (8oz) fine macaroni
50g (2oz) butter
25g (1oz) plain flour
1 small grated onion
5 chicken livers
3 tablespoons brandy

300ml (1/2 pint) chicken or
    vegetable stock
50g (2oz) dried mushrooms,
    soaked and chopped
Salt and pepper

Boil the macaroni until almost tender in plenty of boiling salted water. Grease a timbale mould or soufflé dish and line it with the macaroni.

Melt the butter and lightly brown the onion. Add the flour, stir and simmer for 2 minutes, then add the stock, salt, pepper, chicken livers and mushrooms. Simmer all together for 10 minutes, then add the brandy and pour the sauce into the centre of the timbale. Bake at 190°C/375°F/Gas 5 for 30 minutes.

Macaroni, Neapolitan Style

Maccheroni alla Napoletana

450g (1lb) macaroni
900g (2lb) tomatoes
1 onion, chopped
1 stick celery, chopped
1 carrot, chopped
100g (4oz) diced thick bacon

25g (1oz) butter
Salt and pepper
2 tablespoons chopped fresh basil
1 teaspoon sugar
125ml (4fl oz) olive oil
Fresh Parmesan cheese, grated

Wash, peel and slice the tomatoes. Heat the oil with the bacon and brown the onion, celery and carrot. Add salt, pepper and basil, then the tomatoes. Simmer for 5 minutes, cover with water and continue to simmer for another 40 minutes. Stir and add the butter and sugar. While the sauce is cooking, cook the macaroni in boiling salted water until tender but still firm. Drain in a colander and turn into a deep serving dish. Rub the sauce through a sieve, reheat, and pour it over the macaroni. Serve with grated fresh Parmesan cheese.

Italian cooking

Baked Macaroni

Maccheroni al Forno

Use the rather large macaroni for this dish and cook it in plenty of boiling salted water until it is just tender but not soft. Overcooking turns it soggy.

450g (1lb) large macaroni
100g (4oz) chopped mushrooms
4 sliced tomatoes
Handful of chopped fresh parsley

Salt and pepper
Grated fresh Parmesan cheese
Butter and olive oil
300ml (1/2 pint) béchamel sauce

Heat equal parts of oil and butter and brown the tomatoes, mushrooms and parsley. Add 225ml (8fl oz) of hot water or vegetable stock and simmer until the tomatoes are very soft. Drain the macaroni, pat it dry and turn it into a well-greased oven casserole. Stir in the tomato sauce and the béchamel sauce, this should be very thin, and plenty of grated Parmesan cheese. Add salt and pepper and bake at 190°C/375°F/Gas 5 for 30 minutes.

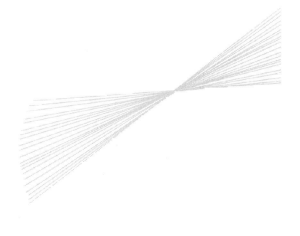

Spaghetti

Spaghetti

Spaghetti, like rice, is a much abused food. Properly cooked and served with a nourishing sauce, which has been well-flavoured, it is a meal in itself. In Italy, however, it is merely something to start a meal with, an antipasto.

450g (1lb) spaghetti   Salt
5.7 litres (10 pints) water

Bring the water, well salted, to the boil and slowly put the spaghetti into it. Keep the spaghetti in its full lengths. It will become limp as soon as it enters the water and it must swim in it. Cook very rapidly, never once letting the water go off the boil. When the spaghetti is al dente, which means cooked through, but firm enough to be felt when bitten, it is done. The time allowed for cooking depends very much on the quality of the spaghetti. Freshly made spaghetti takes only 10 minutes while other varieties take up to 20 minutes.
    When the spaghetti is cooked drain it at once in a colander, then pass it swiftly once under cold running water. Turn it immediately into a serving dish which has been brushed lightly with olive oil and serve as quickly as possible with a sauce and grated fresh Parmesan cheese.

Spaghetti with Anchovies

Spaghetti con le Accuighe

450g (1lb) cooked spaghetti   2 teaspoons tomato purée
100g (4oz) anchovies   Chopped fresh parsley
1 clove garlic, chopped   Grated fresh Parmesan cheese
1 tablespoon olive oil

Wash and chop the anchovies. Heat the oil, then add the garlic and a large handful of chopped parsley. Brown both, and add the anchovies. Simmer for 3 minutes, then add the tomato purée diluted with 125ml (4fl oz) of boiling water. Stir, and pour the sauce over the cooked spaghetti. Serve with grated fresh Parmesan cheese.

Italian cooking

Spaghetti with Fennel, Sicilian Style

Spaghetti e Finocchi alla Siciliana

For this dish you must use the Italian type of fennel which is available from time to time in many grocery shops.

450g (1lb) cooked spaghetti	*100g (4oz) breadcrumbs*
225g (8oz) fennel	*25g (1oz) pine nuts*
4 tablespoons olive oil	*25g (1oz) raisins*
1 onion, chopped	*Black pepper*
450g (1lb) fresh sardines	*Salt*

Smelts, sprats or baby pilchards may be used instead of fresh sardines.

Clean and bone the fish. Wash the fennel and boil it in salt water until tender, about 20 minutes. Cut it into small lengths.

Fry the onion in the oil to a golden brown, add the fish and gently fry them, stirring to prevent sticking. Add the fennel, raisins, pepper and pine nuts and then about 450ml (3/4 pint) of tepid water or white-fish stock. Continue simmering for another 10 minutes.

Pour half the sauce over the cooked spaghetti and sprinkle it with breadcrumbs. Stir well. Serve the spaghetti on individual plates and pour the remaining sauce over it.

Cheese is not added as this is a St Joseph's Day speciality and cheese is not eaten on that day.

Spaghetti with Butter

Spaghetti al Burro

450g (1lb) spaghetti
100g (4oz) butter

75g (3oz) grated fresh Parmesan cheese
Salt to taste

Cook the spaghetti, drain it and place it in individual dishes.

While the spaghetti is cooking heat the butter slowly until it has melted, add salt and pour it immediately over the spaghetti. Sprinkle with grated Parmesan cheese. Garlic lovers can add some crushed garlic to the butter when heating it.

The spaghetti must be piping hot when served this way.

Spaghetti with Meat Sauce

Spaghetti con Carne

450g (1lb) cooked spaghetti
225g (8oz) minced beef or lamb
2 cloves garlic, chopped
50g (2oz) dried and soaked
  mushrooms
1 tablespoon each of fresh
  thyme and parsley
1 onion, chopped
1 small carrot, chopped

1 small turnip, chopped
1 stick celery, chopped
1 small parsnip, chopped
50g (2oz) tomato purée
Salt and pepper
Grated fresh Parmesan cheese
90ml (3fl oz) olive oil
Chicken or vegetable stock

Heat the oil and sauté the meat for a few minutes, then add the garlic and vegetables and brown them slightly. More than cover them with boiling stock. Stir in the tomato purée, add salt, pepper, thyme and parsley. Simmer very gently for 2 hours. Pass through a sieve and reheat. Pour the sauce over the spaghetti. Serve with grated fresh Parmesan cheese.

Italian cooking

Spaghetti with Mariner's Sauce

Spaghetti Marinara

450g (1lb) cooked spaghetti
900g (2lb) tomatoes, chopped
3 onions, chopped
2 cloves garlic, left whole
3 anchovies
1 teaspoon sugar

Pepper
Chopped fresh marjoram
Bacon rinds
50ml (2fl oz) olive oil
Grated fresh Parmesan or
   Romano cheese

Heat the oil and fry the bacon rinds until crisp. Remove rinds and brown the onions and garlic, then add the tomatoes. Simmer for 5 minutes. Remove the garlic and cook slowly for 40 minutes. Stir the tomatoes until very pulpy, add sugar, pepper, marjoram and anchovies, you will not need salt. Simmer for another 15 minutes, then pour the sauce over the cooked spaghetti and serve with grated fresh Parmesan cheese.

Spaghetti, Rice and Noodles
Pasta e Riso

Spaghetti with a Tomato and Red Pepper Sauce

Spaghetti al' Amatriciana

450g (1lb) spaghetti
1 onion
450g (1lb) chopped tomatoes
1 sweet red pepper
1 clove garlic
225g (8oz) cooked minced pork

Handful chopped fresh parsley
50ml (2fl oz) olive oil
Salt and pepper
3 tablespoons grated fresh Parmesan
   or Pecorino cheese

Start cooking the sauce first as it takes longer than the spaghetti. Heat the oil in a pan, brown the garlic, onion and pork. Take out the garlic, add the chopped tomatoes, sliced red pepper and parsley, cook for 5 minutes before adding sufficient hot water or vegetable stock to make a sauce. Add the salt and pepper last. Simmer until the tomatoes are reduced to a pulp, stirring occasionally. The longer you cook the better the flavour, but make sure the sauce does not become too dry.

Cook the spaghetti in the usual way, drain it and mix it well with grated cheese. Pour the sauce over it. Serve extra grated cheese in a deep bowl.

Italian cooking

Spaghetti with Sausage

Spaghetti con Salsiccia

For this dish you can also use *maccheroni rigati*.

450g (1lb) cooked spaghetti
1 small chopped onion
50g (2oz) tomato purée
450g (1lb) Italian pork sausage

150ml (¼ pint) dry white wine
600ml (1 pint) vegetable stock
Butter and olive oil for frying

Slice the sausage into pieces about 2.5cm (1in) thick and brown it with the onion in equal parts olive oil and butter. Add the tomato purée diluted with stock. When this has been well blended with the fat, add the white wine. Simmer for at least 30 minutes, longer if possible. Pour the sauce over the prepared spaghetti. No cheese is required.

Spaghetti with Tuna Fish

Spaghetti con Tonno

Heat 1 tablespoon of olive oil with 1 tablespoon of butter. Brown 2 tablespoons of chopped fresh parsley and 175g (6oz) of chopped tinned tuna fish. Stir a little, but try to avoid breaking up the fish too much, add 225ml (8fl oz) of boiling fish stock or water and simmer gently until the sauce thickens.

Add 150ml (¼ pint) of dry white wine, and pour this sauce over about 450g (1lb) of cooked spaghetti. Serve with grated fresh Parmesan cheese.

Vermicelli with a Clam Sauce

Vermicelli con Vongole

450g (1lb) cooked vermicelli
900g (2lb) clams
2 cloves garlic, chopped
900g (2lb) chopped tomatoes

Chopped fresh parsley to taste
50ml (2fl oz) olive oil
Salt and pepper

Fresh clams are available, but tinned ones are quite good and can be used as well. If you use them, remember that they are already cooked, so that they only need the last minute heating with the sauce.

Cook them in a steamer for 10 minutes, or longer if they have not opened. Strain, save the liquid and take the clams from their shells.

Brown the garlic in oil with the parsley, then add some of the liquid from the clams. Cook for a few minutes, add the tomatoes, chopped and peeled, salt and pepper and cook slowly for 40 minutes. Stir the tomatoes, add the clams and cook for just 2 minutes longer, no more, otherwise the clams will harden.

Cook the vermicelli in exactly the same way as spaghetti.

Vermicelli with Anchovies

Bigoli in Salsa

Heat 1 tablespoon of olive oil and brown 2 chopped cloves of garlic. Add 8 chopped anchovies and simmer for 3 minutes. Stir this sauce into 450g (1lb) of cooked and drained vermicelli.

Italian cooking

Tuscany 'Pancakes'

Cannelloni alla Toscana

450g (1lb) noodle pastry (page 22)   Ravioli filling (pages 37–8)

Roll out the pastry very thinly and cut into pieces 12.5 x 15cm (5 x 6in). Drop these into rapidly boiling salted water and cook for 8 minutes. Remove them one by one with a perforated slice and lay them flat, separately, on a damp cloth. Spread each piece with stuffing and roll up, as you would a pancake. Place in a well-greased casserole and pour over them a sauce, béchamel flavoured with tomato and grated fresh Parmesan cheese is good, and bake at 230°C/450°F/Gas 8 until the sauce is a golden brown colour.

Ravioli Pastry

Ravioli

Originally ravioli were a speciality of Genoa and even today the Genoese ravioli are considered some of the best. Like so many of these pasta recipes they are much simpler to make than one suspects, and naturally there are dozens, probably hundreds, of different ways of filling these little squares of pastry. There are also several recipes for making the dough.

450g (1lb) strong plain white flour   2 eggs   Salt

Sift the flour and the salt together, place on a floured board and drop the eggs in the centre. Work the flour and the eggs together, then add enough water to make a pliable but stiff dough. Knead until smooth, then let it stand for 30 minutes. Cut the dough in half, roll each piece to paper thinness and let it stand for 1 hour to dry.

Drop teaspoons of any filling you prefer on 1 sheet of dough, about 5cm (2in) apart. Cover with another sheet of dough and, with the fingers, gently press around each mound of stuffing. Cut the squares apart with a pastry cutter or very sharp knife and make sure that each ravioli is firmly closed.

Drop into a pan with plenty of rapidly boiling salted water and cook for 8 minutes. Remove carefully and serve with tomato sauce and grated fresh Parmesan cheese.

Italian cooking

Ravioli Pastry with Water

Ravioli

Ravioli pastry can be made, and often is, with water only. While it is obviously not as good as when made with eggs, it is nevertheless quite satisfactory.

Make a firm dough with strong plain white flour and water, add a pinch of salt and knead vigorously until the pastry is pliable. Divide in half and leave it lying in olive oil for 2 hours. You need only a little oil. The pastry should be covered with a cloth during this time and kept warm. When you are satisfied that it is sufficiently pliable, thoroughly wipe all the oil from it, roll it out to paper thinness and leave to dry for 2 hours before using. Use as for egg ravioli pastry above.

Fried Ravioli

Panzarotti alla Napoletana

Make some very small ravioli, any type of filling will do, and fry them in deep boiling fat until an amber colour. Serve hot. Excellent before dinner with cocktails.

Ravioli Filling I (Veal)

Ravioli di Carne

225g (8oz) chopped veal
1 small grated onion
2 whole beaten eggs
100g (4oz) cooked spinach
125ml (4fl oz) red wine
50g (2oz) butter

50g (2oz) grated fresh
  Parmesan cheese
1 slice bread
Salt and pepper
Vegetable stock

Melt the butter, brown the meat then add enough stock to cover the bottom of the pan. Simmer for 20 minutes, add the wine and continue to cook until the meat is tender. Pass through a mincer, combine with the spinach, cheese, onion, bread (soaked in milk and squeezed dry), salt and pepper. Bind with the eggs. Drop on small spoons of the mixture on prepared ravioli pastry.

Ravioli Filling II (Cottage Cheese)

Ravioli di Ricotta

350g (12oz) cottage cheese
1 heaped tablespoon chopped
  fresh parsley
75g (3oz) grated fresh
  Parmesan cheese

1 egg yolk
25g (1oz) butter
Salt and pepper

Whip the butter until smooth, then add the egg yolk. Beat until creamy, then beat into the cottage cheese and continue beating until the texture of the cheese is smooth. Add the chopped fresh parsley and seasoning and drop spoons of the mixture on the prepared ravioli pastry.

Italian cooking

Ravioli Filling III (Spinach)

Ravioli di Spinaci

225g (8oz) cooked spinach	1 egg
Salt and pepper	25g (1oz) butter
50g (2oz) fresh Parmesan cheese	Nutmeg

Chop the spinach very finely and, while still hot, beat in the butter. Add grated Parmesan cheese, or grated Romana cheese, seasonings and a good pinch of nutmeg. Bind with a beaten egg and drop spoons of the mixture on the prepared ravioli pastry.

Sweet Fried Ravioli

Calcionetta

Make a pastry from about 225g (8oz) of well-sieved strong white plain flour, olive oil and dry white wine. The proportion of oil to wine is 1 to 2. Knead it until it is pliable and then wrap it in a cloth and leave it for at least 30 minutes. Divide it into equal halves and roll each half to squares of paper thinness and exactly the same size.

Make a filling from cooked and creamed chestnuts mixed with honey, grated chocolate, grated orange peel and ground almonds. Flavour this mixture with rum and cinnamon and place on the rolled out pastry as if making a savoury ravioli (page 37). Continue as for ravioli but fry the *calcionetta* in deep boiling oil until a golden brown.

Drain them free from surplus oil on absorbent paper, sprinkle with vanilla caster sugar and serve hot.

'Little Hats'

Cappelletti Mantovani

Cappelletti are usually served at Christmas and are not cooked in water but in boiling chicken stock. They are made exactly the same way as *tortellini* (page 40) but folded round an elaborate meat filling in the shape of bowler hats. A filling as for *Ravioli di Carne* would be the best, with plenty of black pepper and rather highly spiced.

Baked Ravioli

Pasticcio di Ravioli

24 ravioli	1 tablespoon tomato purée
175g (6oz) chicken livers, chopped	1 chopped onion
	1 chopped carrot
100g (4oz) cooked minced beef or lamb	1 stick celery, chopped
	150ml (1/4 pint) single cream
75g (3oz) chopped bacon	Salt and pepper
75g (3oz) grated fresh Parmesan cheese	25g (1oz) butter
	Chicken or vegetable stock
75g (3oz) chopped mushrooms	

Cook the ravioli in rapidly boiling water until they are almost al dente (see page 35).

While the ravioli is cooking prepare the sauce. Melt the butter, then lightly fry the onion, carrot and celery. Add the meat, livers, bacon and mushrooms, and cook slowly for 5 minutes. Stir in the tomato purée, add salt and pepper and enough hot stock or water to make a fairly liquid sauce. Add the cream at the last moment.

Drain the ravioli and arrange it in a well-greased flat baking casserole. Cover it with the sauce and sprinkle it with Parmesan cheese. Bake for 15 minutes at at 190°C/375°F/Gas 5.

A second and more simple method is to prepare the ravioli as above, then cover it with a béchamel sauce, faintly coloured with tomato. Add a few very young cooked peas, a little chopped bacon and plenty of grated cheese. Bake for 15 minutes at 190°C/375°F/Gas 5.

Italian cooking

Tortellini

Tortellini alla Bolognese

These are small envelopes, or half-moons, of ravioli pastry with a filling of mixed meat. The pastry used is precisely the same as for ravioli.

450g (1lb) ravioli pastry
100g (4oz) pork
50g (2oz) veal
50g (2oz) mortadella
50g (2oz) turkey
25g (1oz) bacon

100g (4oz) grated fresh
  Parmesan cheese
2 eggs
Salt and pepper
Nutmeg
50g (2oz) butter

Mince the pork, veal, bacon, mortadella and turkey together. Heat the butter and simmer the minced meats until quite cooked. Add cheese, salt, pepper and a good pinch of nutmeg. Cool a little, then bind with the eggs, previously well-beaten.

Roll out the pastry to paper thinness and cut out rounds 5cm (2in) in diameter. Place a spoon of the filling on each round and fold over in the shape of a half-moon. Make sure the edges are firmly closed. Cook and serve in exactly the same way as ravioli. The above quantities make about 80 tortellini.

Boiled Rice for Risottos

Risotto in 'Cagnoni'

It is relatively simple to serve rice that is perfectly cooked with each grain separate yet soft all through. The best rice for risottos and Italian savoury dishes is long-grain. Put the rice slowly into plenty of rapidly boiling water flavoured with lemon juice and let it continue to boil quickly for 10 to 15 minutes. Using a wooden fork, take out a few grains to taste. If they are cooked through, immediately remove the pan from the heat, drain the rice and put it into a well-greased dish. Dry in a warm, not hot, oven (180°C/350°F/Gas 4). Stir it occasionally with a wooden fork.

Rice Cooked with Fish Stock

Risotto col Brodo di Pesce

Heat 50g (2oz) of butter in a pan and brown 1 small chopped onion, a sliced clove of garlic, a stick of celery broken into small pieces, a sliced carrot and 2 tablespoons of chopped fresh parsley. Add 225g (8oz) of rice, simmer for 10 minutes, then add 1.2 litres (2 pints) of fish stock. Season with salt and pepper, cover tightly and leave over the lowest possible heat until the liquid is absorbed.

Stir in 25g (1oz) of butter before serving and sprinkle with grated fresh Parmesan cheese.

Rice with Crayfish

Risotto con Scampi

If you buy your crayfish uncooked, first cook them in plenty of cold water to which 225ml (8fl oz) of dry white wine, some chopped celery or celery leaves, 1 carrot and 1 onion have been added. When the crayfish turn pink, take them from the heat. Peel the fish and pick out the flesh. Put the better pieces aside and rub the rest through a sieve. Strain the stock.

Melt 50g (2oz) of butter, brown 1 finely chopped onion, a chopped stick of celery, a chopped clove of garlic and a handful of chopped fresh parsley. Add 225g (8oz) of long-grain rice and simmer until the rice looks transparent. Pour over it 1.2 litres (2 pints) of strained fish stock and add the sieved crayfish. Stir, then cover tightly and simmer until all the liquid is absorbed. Season with a generous amount of black pepper and flavour with plenty of grated fresh Parmesan cheese. Remove from the heat. Mix in the rest of the crayfish, or pile this in a heap on top of the rice.

This recipe can be used with lobster, prawns or shrimps, and can be adapted without difficulty to tinned fish of this type.

If you buy cooked crayfish, remove the flesh from the shells and make a stock by simmering the shells for 1 hour in water to which dry white wine, chopped celery, a carrot and an onion have been added. Then continue as above.

Italian cooking

Rice, Milanese Style

Risotto Milanese

450g (1lb) long-grain rice
1 small onion, chopped
100g (4oz) butter
1/2 teaspoon saffron

Salt and pepper
1.7 litres (3 pints) boiling
  vegetable stock
100g (4oz) grated fresh Parmesan
  cheese

Melt the butter in a large saucepan, add the onion and when it starts to brown throw in the rice. Fry until the rice looks transparent, stirring frequently to prevent sticking. Add the stock, salt, pepper and saffron. Mix well, cover and cook over the lowest possible heat until the rice has absorbed all the liquid. Just before serving stir in the cheese and a knob of butter.

   Note: When simmering the rice in the stock cover the saucepan first with a cloth then with a lid. This ensures the rice will absorb the liquid and be free of starch; and the result will be well-separated grains. This is a trick that I learnt in Turkey, not in Italy.

Rice with Chicken Livers

Risotto alla Finanziera

Heat 100g (4oz) of butter and very lightly fry 1 finely chopped onion and as many chicken livers as you require. Add a few chopped mushrooms, half a chopped red pepper, salt, pepper and, lastly, 450g (1lb) of long-grain rice. Fry for 15 minutes, stirring constantly, then add 1.2 litres (2 pints) of boiling chicken stock and 150ml (1/4 pint) of Marsala or sherry. Cover very tightly and leave on the lowest possible heat until all the liquid is absorbed. Serve with grated fresh Parmesan cheese.

Mushrooms with Rice

Risotto con Funghi

Prepared as *Risotto Milanese* (see page 42), omitting the saffron and substituting mushrooms. Fry these with the onion before the rice.

Tomatoes with Rice

Risotto Pomidoro

Cook 225g (8oz) of long-grain rice in 600ml (1 pint) of vegetable stock until tender, stir into it a well-flavoured tomato sauce (pages 216–7) and sprinkle well with grated fresh Parmesan cheese.

Timbale of Rice

Timballo di Riso (Sartu)

Sartu, as this timbale is called in Naples, is a name of unknown origin.
    First make a plain risotto, using 450g (1lb) of long-grain rice.
    Heat 1 tablespoon of olive oil, add 1 finely chopped onion and when this is a pale golden colour add 1 peeled and chopped tomato, 25g (1oz) of dried mushrooms, soaked and well washed, 4 chicken livers, salt and pepper. Simmer for 5 minutes then add 150ml (1/4 pint) of chicken stock and the same quantity of dry white wine. Simmer for another 15 minutes stirring everything well together.
    Grease a mould and sprinkle it lightly with fine breadcrumbs. Fill it with the rice, mixed with 1 tablespoon of the sauce, two chopped hard-boiled eggs and plenty of grated fresh Parmesan cheese. Put it in a very slow oven (150°C/300°F/Gas 2) for 1 hour then turn it out. It should have a light golden crust. Serve it with some of the sauce as a garnish, and put the rest of the sauce in a sauce boat.

Italian cooking

Semolina Gnocchi

Gnocchi alla Romana

600ml (1 pint) milk
100g (4oz) semolina
2 beaten eggs

Grated nutmeg
Butter
Salt and pepper

Bring the milk to the boil then add the semolina. Flavour with grated nutmeg, season with salt and pepper and cook slowly for 5 minutes, or until the semolina thickens, stirring all the time. Remove the semolina from the heat and quickly whip in the eggs. Pour the mixture into a well-greased flat tin and smooth it out to about 1cm (1/2in) in thickness. Leave to get quite cold.

Cut into squares and arrange these in a greased flat casserole. Sprinkle very liberally with cheese and dot with thin slivers of butter. Brown at 230°C/450°F/Gas 8. Grated fresh Parmesan cheese and a tomato sauce should be served separately with the gnocchi.

Potato Gnocchi

Gnocchi alla Piemontese

900g (2lb) floury potatoes
350g (12oz) plain flour

Grated fresh Parmesan cheese
Salt

Boil the potatoes until they are very soft and pass through a sieve. Mix with the flour and work into a smooth and manageable dough. Roll the dough with the palms of the hands into a strip. Cut into 2cm (3/4in) cubes. Press your thumb into the middle of each piece and drop, one by one, into boiling salted water and cook for 10 minutes. Drain and serve with a tomato sauce and grated fresh Parmesan cheese.

Sweet Fried Semolina Gnocchi

La Frittura Dolce

600ml (1 pint) milk
100g (4oz) semolina
2 eggs
Lemon juice
25g (1oz) sugar

Butter
1–2 beaten eggs
Plain flour
Breadcrumbs

Bring the milk to the boil, throw in the semolina and cook it, stirring all the time, until it is very thick. Beat the eggs until frothy, with a few drops of lemon juice and the sugar. Whip this quickly into the semolina. Pour the mixture on to a well-greased board and smooth it out till it is 1cm (1/2in) thick. Leave to cool, then cut into small squares, roll in flour, egg and breadcrumbs and fry quickly in butter. Serve sprinkled with sugar.

An alternative method is to omit the sugar and lemon and serve with grated fresh Parmesan cheese and tomato sauce.

Italian cooking

Cornmeal

Polenta

This is finely ground Italian wheat corn and used much in Italian cooking.
Properly prepared it can be most satisfying.

450g (1lb) polenta   2.3 litres (4 pints) boiling water
2 teaspoons salt

When the water is bubbling add the salt, then gradually the cornmeal,
stirring vigorously all the time to prevent it becoming lumpy. Once the
cornmeal has been smoothed out and well-stirred it can be left to cook for
30 to 40 minutes in an ordinary saucepan, or for 1½ hours in a double
boiler. When the polenta is ready it should have the consistency of a thick
purée and come away from the sides of the pan easily.
    Serve in a large flat dish, sprinkle with salt and pepper and pour a
rich tomato or mushroom sauce over it. Sprinkle with grated fresh
Parmesan cheese.

Baked Cornmeal Pie

Pasticcio di Polenta

Prepare the cornmeal as in preceding recipe then pour it into a round
greased casserole. Leave it until it has quite set, then turn it out and slice into
3 layers. Regrease the casserole, return the bottom layer of polenta and
spread this with a thick mushroom sauce and sprinkle with grated fresh
Parmesan cheese, slivers of butter, salt and cayenne pepper. Cover with the
second layer and repeat the mushroom sauce etc., then add the third layer.
Brush lightly with butter, sprinkle with grated fresh Parmesan cheese and
bake at 190°C/375°F/Gas 5 for 1 hour.
    Serve with a mushroom sauce and grated fresh Parmesan cheese.
    If available, make the mushroom sauce with Italian dried mushrooms,
they have a strong flavour which goes well with the cornmeal.

_____

Soup
Le Minestre

Italian cooking

Almond and Rice Soup, Sicilian Style

Minestra alla Siciliana

50g (2oz) sweet almonds
1.4 litres (2¹/2 pints) milk
150g (5oz) long-grain rice

2 egg yolks
50g (2oz) butter
Salt

Blanch and finely chop the almonds. Cook in 300ml (¹/2 pint) of milk for about 15 minutes.

In another saucepan bring some water to a rapid boil, add the rice and cook it until it is soft. Then drain off the water, add the remaining milk and bring to the boil once more. Add the almonds and the milk in which they have been cooking, and continue to cook for 5 minutes. Then pass everything through a sieve.

Return the soup to the pan, add the butter in small pieces and stir it in, add a pinch of salt and remove the pan from the heat. Beat the egg yolks until smooth and then quickly whisk them into the rice mixture. Serve hot.

Sweet soups are popular in various parts of Europe and are eaten like other soups, at the start of a meal.

Italian cooking

Dr Arnaldi's Soup

Minestrone all' Arnaldi

This soup, which is both nourishing and light, is reputed to have been one of the specialities of the famous Italian dietitian, Dr Carlo Arnaldi, who would order it for his patients to build up their strength.

Wash about 1.4kg (3lb) of mixed green vegetables such as spinach, turnip tops, lettuce and celery tops, and cook them without any more water than that which adheres to their leaves. Add a handful of chopped fresh parsley, a very finely chopped or grated onion and some fresh herbs, salt and pepper.

When the vegetables are soft, chop them and rub them through a sieve. Return to the pan with 600ml (1 pint) of vegetable stock, and continue to cook until the liquid is reduced by half. This soup should be thickish but not a cream. Drop an egg into a soup bowl and pour the very hot soup over it. Leave it to settle for a minute or so, then serve. The egg will be sufficiently cooked for eating.

Roman Bean Soup

Zuppa di Fagioli alla Romana

225g (8oz) red beans
Stick celery, chopped
1 carrot, chopped
1 large onion, chopped
225g (8oz) tomatoes, chopped
2 tablespoons fresh parsley,
  chopped

2 cloves garlic, chopped
1 tablespoon olive oil
Fresh rosemary, chopped
100g (4oz) long-grain rice
Salt and pepper
Bicarbonate of soda

Soak the beans overnight, then put them into a pan with plenty of water. Add the chopped vegetables, except the tomatoes, and a good pinch of soda and cook until tender, about 2 1/2 hours.

Heat the oil and slowly simmer the garlic, parsley and tomatoes until the latter are soft. Add some chopped rosemary, salt and pepper, and stir this mixture into the beans about 30 minutes before they are tender. About 5 minutes before the end of cooking time, take out about half the beans. Pass the rest of the soup through a sieve. Return to the pan and bring to the boil, then throw in the rice. Cook for a further 15 minutes, or until the rice is soft. Just before serving return the cup of beans to the soup. Serve in earthenware soup bowls and sprinkle with grated fresh Parmesan cheese.

Like so many Italian soups this would not be considered a soup in Britain because it is so thick. But it is very nourishing and excellent on a cold night.

The flavour is considerably improved if a piece of salt pork, bacon or even bacon rind is added to the beans. It should be removed before serving.

Italian cooking

Chestnut Soup

Zuppa di Castagne

450g (1lb) chestnuts
600ml (1 pint) milk
1 minced onion
50g (2oz) butter
Plain flour
Handful celery leaves, chopped

1 teaspoon salt
Pinch nutmeg
225ml (8fl oz) single cream
Chopped fresh parsley
Pepper
Croutons

If you have no celery leaves use about 1/4 teaspoon of celery salt. If you use celery leaves, chop them very finely.

Slit the chestnuts, roast or boil them until you are able to remove the outer shell and the inner skin with ease. Return them to the pan, and cook them until they are soft. Pass through a fine sieve and mix with the milk. Melt the butter in a deep pan, and very lightly fry the onion until soft, but not brown. Sprinkle with flour and stir. Add the salt, pepper, nutmeg and celery leaves (actually celery salt is easier). When all these ingredients are well blended, gradually add the chestnut and milk mixture, stirring all the while.

Cook slowly for 10 minutes, then add the cream. Bring once more to boiling point and quickly remove from the heat. Garnish with finely chopped fresh parsley and serve very hot with croutons.

Broth from Chickens' Feet

Zuppa di Zampe di Pollo

6 pairs chicken feet
2 sticks celery, chopped
1 carrot, chopped
2 leeks, chopped

1 beaten egg yolk
Salt and pepper
2 tablespoons olive oil
Bacon rinds

Continental cooks use parts of the chicken that we are apt to throw away. It should be easy enough to persuade your poulterer to provide you with chickens' feet with which to make this soup.

Wash the feet and singe them long enough to be able to remove the skin and claws with ease.

Heat the oil and brown the bacon rinds together with the vegetables. Add the legs, brown them, then pour in about 1.7 litres (3 pints) of boiling water. Flavour with salt and pepper and cook fairly slowly until you have a well flavoured broth. Strain through a fine sieve, beat in the egg yolk, gently reheat and serve with croutons or semolina dumplings (page 54).

Broth with Curd Dumplings

Bomboline di Ricotta in Brodo

175g (6oz) cottage cheese
2 eggs
75g (3oz) plain flour
Nutmeg

Salt and pepper
1.7 litres (3 pints) hot vegetable stock
Chopped fresh parsley
Olive oil

Beat the cheese with a wooden spoon until it is creamy, then add the flour, eggs, a pinch of ground nutmeg, salt (not much of this) and pepper. Mix to a firm paste and shape into small dumplings. Leave for 30 minutes in a cool place.

Roll the dumplings in flour, and fry first until they are golden brown in hot oil, and then drop them into a pan of boiling vegetable stock and let them cook rapidly for 2 minutes. Sprinkle the broth with finely chopped fresh parsley just before serving.

Italian cooking

Broth with Eggs

Zuppa alla Pavese

1 egg per person
Grated fresh Parmesan cheese
Fried bread

Salt and pepper
Chicken stock

Place in each soup bowl a slice of bread and sprinkle with cheese. Drop on to each piece of bread 1 raw egg, taking care not to break the yolk, and sprinkle it with salt and pepper. Pour boiling chicken stock over the egg and almost fill the bowl. By the time you have brought the soup to the table the egg will have set. Serve at once.

Broth with Semolina Dumplings

Chenelle di Semolino

50g (2oz) semolina
2 eggs
Salt and pepper
Nutmeg

25g (1oz) butter
1.2 litres (2 pints) boiling
  vegetable stock

Soften the butter and then beat it with the eggs until it is creamy. Add the salt, pepper and a pinch of nutmeg. Gradually stir in the semolina, making quite sure that the mixture is well-blended.

Have ready a pan filled with boiling water. Drop small spoons of semolina into this. The semolina will swell and should look like tiny eggs. Cook for 2 minutes, then drain from the water and drop into a saucepan of boiling vegetable stock. Cook for 2 more minutes, then serve the broth with the dumplings.

Onion Soup

Zuppa di Cipolla

900g (2lb) chopped onions
25g (1oz) plain flour
50g (2oz) grated fresh
 Parmesan cheese
Salt and pepper

1.7 litres (3 pints) chicken or
 vegetable stock
1 tablespoon olive oil
Small croutons
Gruyère cheese

Heat the oil and fry the onions to a golden brown. Mix the flour to a paste with a little milk (or water) and pour this over the onions. Stir and cool for 2 minutes. Gradually add the stock and continue stirring for 2 minutes. Cook gently for another 30 minutes, and then pass the mixture through a sieve. Return to the pan, add the Parmesan cheese and about 12 small cubes of Gruyère cheese. Stir again for 1 to 2 minutes until all the ingredients are well-mixed. Add salt and pepper.

Serve the soup piping hot, preferably in French-type potage bowls, adding croutons.

Egg and Cheese Consommé

Consomme all' Uovo

Break into a bowl as many eggs as you need using one for each person. Add the juice of ¼ lemon to each egg and beat until smooth. Add some hot, but not boiling, vegetable stock and gradually thin the egg and lemon mixture. Season with salt and pepper and reheat very cautiously, taking care to keep the eggs from curdling. Add enough grated fresh Parmesan cheese to give a good flavour and serve with fried croutons.

Tinned chicken consommé is excellent for this soup. The number of eggs can be reduced but not too greatly, as this would spoil the soup.

Italian cooking

Creamed Onion Soup

Passato di Cipolla

Stew about 450–900g (1–2lb) of onions in water until they are very soft. Add salt and pepper and then pass them through a sieve. Beat in plenty of grated fresh Parmesan cheese, an egg and a knob of butter. Reheat and serve hot with fried triangles of bread. This soup should be very thick and white.

Milanese Soup

Minestrone Alla Milanese

225g (8oz) dried mixed beans
2 potatoes, chopped
2 tomatoes, chopped
2 courgettes chopped
2 carrots, chopped
1/2 small cabbage, chopped
1 stick celery, chopped
1 onion, chopped
pinch fresh sage

Handful fresh peas
100g (4oz) long-grain rice
75g (3oz) butter
25g (1oz) bacon rinds
1 clove garlic, chopped
75g (3oz) grated fresh Parmesan
  cheese
Salt and pepper

Soak the beans overnight and cook them next day until they are almost tender. Strain.

Melt the butter and crisp the bacon rinds. Remove the rinds, then add the vegetables and the garlic to the fat and fry lightly. Pour into the pan about 2.3 litres (4 pints) of boiling water. Bring slowly to the boil, then add the beans and cook for 10 minutes. Add the rice, salt, pepper and sage and cook for a further 15 minutes. Sprinkle the soup with the cheese before serving and stir well.

Paradise Soup

Minestra paradiso

2 egg yolks
2 egg whites
50g (2oz) white breadcrumbs
50g (2oz) grated fresh
  Parmesan cheese

Salt and pepper
Nutmeg
25g (1oz) butter
1.7 litres (3 pints) hot
  vegetable stock

Beat the yolks with salt and pepper and a pinch of nutmeg until very light and frothy. Beat the whites to a meringue consistency.

Sauté the breadcrumbs in butter until golden. Remove from the heat and stir in the cheese and the beaten yolks. Stir until everything is well-blended and then add the egg whites and 150ml (1/4 pint) of the stock. Mix well, and then pour this mixture into the rest of the stock, stirring vigorously all the time to prevent the eggs or the cheese from curdling. Add seasoning and nutmeg, bring the stock once to the boil and serve the soup immediately.

Creamed Pea Soup

Crema di Piselli

1.4kg (3lb) fresh peas
1.7 litres (3 pints) vegetable
  stock

Croutons
Grated fresh Parmesan cheese
15g (1/2oz) butter

Shell the peas and cook them in the stock until they are soft. Pass through a sieve. Return to the pan and stir in the butter. Beat until smooth. Serve hot, sprinkled with grated Parmesan cheese and with very small croutons. This soup should be almost as thick as a purée.

This recipe can also be used for almost all of the root vegetables, dried beans and peas, and is particularly good for use with chick-peas. Always add a really good pinch of soda when soaking dried beans, etc.

Italian cooking

Rice and Lemon Soup

Minestrina di Riso al Limone

175g (6oz) long-grain rice
50g (2oz) grated fresh Parmesan
  cheese

2.3 litres (4 pints) vegetable stock
2 egg yolks
Juice 1/2 lemon

Bring the stock to the boil, throw in the rice and cook rapidly for 20 minutes. Beat the egg yolks, add the cheese, gradually pour in the lemon juice and stir this mixture into the soup just before serving. Serve at once.

Rice and Pea Soup

Risi e Bisi

This soup, even thicker than most Italian soups, was considered by the Venetians as their soup *par excellence*. It was always served by the Doges of Venice at banquets given on the Feast of Saint Mark. I suspect no one was able to eat much after a generous helping of *Risi e Bisi*. As with all traditional dishes, there are several ways to prepare this soup, all arriving at approximately the same result. Here are two recipes.

1. Fry lightly in butter some bacon rinds, a chopped carrot, a chopped onion, a stick of chopped celery and about 225g (8oz) of shelled green peas. Remove the rinds, add about 1.7 litres (3 pints) of hot vegetable stock, and then throw in 225g (8oz) of long-grain rice. Cook rapidly until the rice is tender, add salt and pepper and serve very hot and thick.

2. Or you can reverse the process. Fry the bacon and chopped vegetables until brown. Add the rice, and when this becomes transparent, about 5 minutes' frying will be enough, pour in the hot stock. Add the peas and tightly cover the pan. Simmer the rice and peas over the lowest possible heat, and leave until both are soft. Remove the rinds before serving.

This soup one eats with a fork and not a spoon. It should be basically rice, with a green motif.

Peasant Soup

Zuppa Rustica

1 cabbage
3 leeks
2 carrots
1 large onion
3 potatoes
450g (1lb) peas
225g (8oz) broad beans

100g (4oz) chopped bacon
6 small Italian sausages
100g (4oz) black sausage
Salt and pepper
Grated fresh cheese
Croutons

Wash and prepare all the vegetables and chop all but the peas and beans into small pieces. Put the vegetables, with the black sausage and the bacon, into a saucepan with about 2.3 litres (4 pints) of water. Simmer for 2 hours. About 15 minutes before the soup is ready add the small sausages. Serve unstrained with an abundance of grated cheese and croutons.

The cheese intended for this peasant soup is one which comes from the Lombardy district, but any strongly flavoured cheese may be used.

Italian cooking

Potato Soup

Zuppa di Patate

700g (1 1/2 lb) potatoes
1 onion, finely chopped
1 carrot, finely chopped
1 stick celery, finely chopped
2 cloves garlic, finely chopped
Handful fresh parsley, finely
  chopped
25g (1oz) bacon, finely chopped

900ml (1 1/2 pints) milk
600ml (1 pint) water
1 egg
25g (1oz) butter
2 tablespoons olive oil
Grated fresh Parmesan cheese
Croutons

Boil the peeled potatoes in 1.2 litres (2 pints) mixed milk and water, half of each, until they are soft enough to be mashed to a cream. Beat in the butter and the egg. Reheat and stir in the rest of the milk.

While the potatoes are cooking, fry all the vegetables and bacon in oil with the garlic and the parsley. Stir this mixture into the potatoes. When the soup is in the plates, sprinkle with grated Parmesan cheese and serve with crisply fried croutons.

This version of potato soup, like so many other Italian soups, is very thick, rather like a purée of potatoes, and is very substantial.

Semolina Soup

Zuppa di Semolino

75g (3oz) semolina
2–3 eggs
1.7 litres (3 pints) vegetable stock

Grated fresh Parmesan cheese
Ground nutmeg
Salt

Beat the eggs until they are smooth, then add the semolina. You need to make a paste which is neither too firm nor too runny. Add salt and a good quantity of nutmeg, for this soup needs plenty of flavouring.

Bring the stock to the boil, then slowly pour it on to the semolina paste, stirring all the while. Return the thickened stock to the pan, add 3 tablespoons of Parmesan cheese, and cook for 5 minutes stirring continually. Serve very hot.

Spinach Soup

Zuppa di Spinaci

900g (2lb) spinach
Butter
1.2 litres (2 pints) vegetable stock
2 tablespoons milk

Salt and pepper
Nutmeg
Croutons

Wash and thoroughly pick over the spinach. Shake dry and chop. Melt about 25g (1oz) of butter in a saucepan and gently simmer the spinach until soft. Add salt and pepper and a good pinch of nutmeg. Gradually pour in the stock and milk, stirring all the time, and immediately before serving add 2 tablespoons of croutons.

A little well-flavoured pâté or anchovy paste mixed with the butter gives a slightly different flavour and is an improvement.

Consommé Stracciatella

Stracciatella

3 eggs
75g (3oz) semolina
75g (3oz) grated fresh
  Parmesan cheese

1.7 litres (3 pints) vegetable stock
Nutmeg
Salt

Break the eggs into a bowl and add the semolina, cheese, nutmeg, salt and 150ml (1/4 pint) of the liquid. Beat until smooth. Bring the remaining liquid to the boil, and gradually add the semolina mixture, whisking briskly all the while to prevent the eggs or cheese from curdling. Simmer very gently for 4 to 5 minutes, no longer, stirring all the time.

This is a famous Italian soup, and very simple; yet it is not easy to guess just what makes it so good for its flavour is undefinable.

Italian cooking

Consommé Zanzarelle

Zanzarelle

6 tablespoons plain flour
3 eggs
Salt and pepper

Nutmeg
1.7 litres (3 pints) vegetable stock
Grated fresh Parmesan cheese

Beat the eggs and pour into a pan with a lip. Put the pan over a low heat and gradually add the flour. Simmer, stirring all the time, until you have a smooth paste of pouring consistency neither too thin nor too thick. You may have to add just a little milk. Flavour with nutmeg and season with salt and pepper.

Bring the stock to the boil, then immediately lower the heat. Gradually pour in the paste in such a way that it falls like long strings of vermicelli.

The easiest way to do this is to make some very neat holes in the bottom of a clean tin, and pour the paste through this. Stir the stock to give the paste a chance to move around, and when you have exhausted the paste add some grated Parmesan cheese and cook fairly rapidly for 5 minutes.

Genoese Soup with Garlic Paste

Zuppa di Pesto

Prepare a vegetable soup using shredded cabbage, courgettes, green beans, peas, potatoes, tomatoes, etc. Just before it is ready stir into it a garlic paste or pesto. There are several recipes for making pesto, but probably the following recipe is one of the best. Chop 3 cloves of garlic together with 4 tablespoons of finely chopped fresh basil and a little salt. When these ingredients are well-crushed, add 2 tablespoons of grated fresh Parmesan cheese. Mix with just enough good olive oil to make a smooth fairly liquid paste.

Creamed Tomato Soup

Zuppa Crema di Pomidoro

8 tomatoes
25g (1oz) flour
1 large onion, chopped
1 tablespoon fresh
  parsley, chopped

Salt, pepper and sugar
1.2 litres (2 pints) vegetable stock
125ml (4fl oz) single cream
Butter
Parmesan fingers (page 13)

Sauté the onion in butter, then sprinkle in the flour. Stir well and continue cooking for 3 minutes, but take care that the onion does not brown. Add the tomatoes, peeled and chopped, salt and pepper, a good pinch of sugar and the parsley. Simmer until the tomatoes are very soft. Pour in the hot stock and continue cooking for another 15 minutes. Rub everything through a sieve, stir in a knob of butter and the cream. Serve with Parmesan fingers (page 13).

Italian cooking

Turnip Soup

Zuppa di Rape

900g (2lb) turnips	Sliced stale bread
75g (3oz) streaky bacon	Grated fresh Parmesan cheese
50g (2oz) butter	Salt and pepper
1 small onion, chopped	

Peel and slice the turnips. Melt the butter and fry the chopped onion and the bacon. Remove the bacon when crisp. Add the turnips and brown them lightly, and then gradually pour in 1.7 litres (3 pints) of boiling water. Add salt and pepper and cook until the turnips are soft. Strain, but reserve the liquid keeping it very hot.

Arrange a layer of turnips at the bottom of a soup tureen and cover with a layer of bread. Repeat these layers until all the turnips are used up. Between each layer sprinkle pepper and grated Parmesan cheese. Pour in the liquid and serve immediately.

The bread should be very thinly sliced and the crusts removed.

Use a light vegetable stock instead of water, it makes the soup more nourishing and the flavour is better.

Crayfish Soup

Zuppa di Gamberi

24 live crayfish (Dublin Bay
  prawns)
2 carrots, chopped
2 sticks celery, chopped
1 tablespoon fresh parsley,
  chopped
125ml (4fl oz) brandy or Marsala
125ml (4fl oz) dry white wine

100g (4oz) long-grain rice
1 tablespoon tomato purée
1 bay leaf
25g (1oz) butter
Salt and pepper
3 peppercorns
Celery leaves

Drop the crayfish into a pan with plenty of boiling water adding a bay leaf, a handful of celery leaves and the peppercorns. After 5 minutes' cooking, take out the fish and remove the shells. (Pinch with a quick movement the extreme end of the centre fin and take out the intestines and the cyst.) Strain the liquid and reserve it.

Melt the butter in a saucepan and then brown the vegetables and the crayfish. Dilute the tomato purée with 600ml (1 pint) of the fish liquid. Pour this into the pan, then add the dry white wine and parsley. Cook until the crayfish are very soft. Pour in the brandy or Marsala, and continue cooking for a few minutes.

Take the crayfish out of the pan with a perforated spoon and mash them together with the rice. Reduce both to a paste, and stir this back into the soup. Add salt and pepper, stir well and then as quickly as possible pass everything through a sieve. Reheat and serve hot with snippets of fried bread. If too thick add a little more of the crayfish stock.

Italian cooking

Eel Soup

Zuppa di Ceci

This traditional soup hails from the Lombardy district and is eaten with unfailing regularity on 2 November, All Souls' Day.

1 large eel	*2 carrots, chopped*
25g (1oz) butter	*1 stick celery, chopped*
1 small onion, chopped	*450g (1lb) salt pork*
1 clove garlic, chopped	*6 slices toast*
1 tablespoon fresh parsley,	*Salt and pepper*
chopped	

Soak the eel in plenty of water for 24 hours. Cut it into 5cm (2in) lengths.

Melt the butter in a saucepan and lightly fry the onion, garlic, parsley, carrots and celery. Add enough boiling water to nearly fill the pan. Bring to the boil, add the eel and cook this for 1 hour before adding the meat. Continue cooking for 1½ hours. Add salt and pepper. Remove the meat, take from it any bone and cut it into shreds. Return the meat to the soup and continue cooking until it is reheated.

Put the toast in the bottom of a soup tureen, pour the soup over it and serve everything as hot as possible.

Fish Soup

La Burrida

Writers, as well as cooks, have waxed lyrical on the subject of bouillabaisse, and, while it is generally claimed to have its origin in Marseilles, my Italian friends insist that it belongs just as much to their country.

It is difficult to make a really good *burrida* in Britain as the fish required belong properly to more exotic waters than ours. However, a reasonable imitation can be prepared by using gurnet, whiting, haddock, eel, bream, turbot, brill and as many kinds of fish as possible.

1.4kg (3lb) mixed fish	*1 bay leaf*
2 large onions, chopped	*Saffron*
3 tomatoes, chopped	*1 piece orange peel*
1 head fennel, chopped	*125ml (4fl oz) olive oil*
6 cloves garlic, chopped	*6 slices fried bread*
Fresh parsley, chopped	*25g (1oz) butter*

Heat half the oil in a saucepan and lightly brown the onions and garlic. Add the fennel, parsley, bay leaf, orange peel and the tomatoes. Leave to simmer gently while preparing the fish.

Clean and trim the fish and cut into 5cm (2in) lengths. Divide the coarse fish from the more delicate. First add the coarser fish to the simmering vegetables, season with salt and pepper and cover with boiling water. Cook on a fast heat for 5 minutes, then add the rest of the oil, a good pinch of saffron and, lastly, the remainder of the fish. Bring once more to the boil, add the butter, and continue cooking quickly until all the fish is tender. Strain off the fish and arrange on a dish.

Have ready in large soup plates some slices of crisply fried bread. Pour the soup over this. Serve the fish at the same time as the soup. It is usual to eat the soup first, and the fish afterwards, using the same plate. However, there is nothing against eating the soup and the fish together.

The point of the quick boiling is to ensure that the oil and the water blend thoroughly. Take care that the fish is not overcooked, otherwise it will disintegrate. Usually 15 minutes is enough to cook the fish, but it depends largely on the quality.

Italian cooking

Fish Soup with Noodles

Brodo di Pesce con Tagliatelle

900g (2lb) fish
1 onion, chopped
1 carrot, chopped
2 sticks celery, chopped
3 tomatoes, chopped

Grated fresh Parmesan cheese
50ml (2fl oz) olive oil
100g (4oz) noodles
Salt and pepper

An economical recipe, for you may have fish soup one day and mayonnaise of fish the next. Select firm, white fish such as haddock, whiting or fresh cod.

Clean and trim the fish but leave whole. Heat the oil in a large saucepan, then lightly fry the onion, carrot and celery. Add the tomatoes, lower the heat and simmer until the tomatoes begin to soften. Add salt and pepper, then pour in about 2.3 litres (4 pints) of boiling water. Cook gently for another 20 minutes, then add the fish. Continue cooking fairly gently until the fish is tender. Remove it carefully and put aside for later use.

Strain the stock and vegetables through a sieve and return at once to the pan. Bring quickly to the boil, then throw in the noodles. Cook over a good heat for 15 minutes, and serve very hot, sprinkled with grated Parmesan cheese.

If you are not using a fish kettle, it is a good idea to wrap the fish in clean buttered muslin and cook it in this so that you can remove it easily. Provided the muslin is washed and absolutely clean it will not affect the flavour.

Fish Soup, Leghorn Style

Cacciucco Livornese

This is a famous Italian dish and considered one of the glories of Mediterranean cooking. Italian cooks preparing it will give full rein to their inventive powers and imagination, and their choice of fish will include octopus, eels (large and small), mullet, racasse, a species of fish unobtainable here, and also a kind of waterhen, as well as other fish for which I do not know the English names. However, a passable imitation can be made by using as many different kinds of fish as possible. Each will give to the stew its different flavour. All the fish should be cleaned and trimmed and cut into small pieces.

1.4kg (3lb) mixed fish
1 whole head celery, chopped
4 large onions, chopped
450g (1lb) tomatoes, chopped
3 cloves garlic, chopped
Ginger and fresh marjoram
   to taste

Lemon juice
150ml (¼ pint) dry white wine
125ml (4fl oz) olive oil
Salt and pepper
1 chilli pepper
Boiling water
6 slices very crisp toast

Season all the fish with salt and pepper, and sprinkle with lemon juice. Heat the oil in a deep pan and fry all the vegetables and 1 clove of garlic until brown. Add the fish, pour in the wine, and simmer until the wine has almost evaporated. Add boiling water to cover, ginger, marjoram and chilli pepper, and bring once to the boil. Continue cooking over a fairly good heat until all the fish is tender.

   Pound the remaining garlic and smear this over the toast. Arrange the toast at the bottom of a soup tureen, cover it with the strained fish, and then pour in the liquid. Serve this stew piping hot and as soon as possible after pouring the liquid into the tureen.

Italian cooking

Frogs' Legs Soup

Zuppa di Rane

In Italy this soup is considered a delicacy, as indeed it should be, for the flavour of frogs is very similar to that of chicken. The hind legs only are used. If not already prepared, these must be cut from the body, washed thoroughly in cold water, and the skin stripped off. It comes off easily, like a glove.

6 pairs frogs' legs
2 tablespoons olive oil
1 small onion, chopped
1 stick celery, chopped
1 carrot, chopped
Handful fresh parsley, chopped

3 tomatoes, chopped
1 clove garlic, chopped
Salt and pepper
1.7 litres (3 pints) chicken stock
Croutons

Season the frogs' legs with plenty of salt and black pepper. Heat the oil in a deep pan, fry the onion and the other vegetables (except the tomatoes) and then the legs until they are a golden brown. Add the parsley, garlic and then tomatoes and simmer until these are very soft, about 30 minutes. Pour in the stock, cook for a further 30 minutes, then pass everything through a sieve, pressing the legs well down with a mallet in order to get all the flavour from them into the soup. Return to the pan, reheat, then serve with the croutons.

Fish Stew, Trieste Style

Brodetto alla Triestina

1.4kg (3lb) mixed fish
1 tablespoon tomato purée
1 clove garlic, chopped
1 large onion, chopped

1 tablespoon vinegar
Handful of chopped fresh parsley
125ml (4fl oz) olive oil
Croutons

Cheaper cuts of fish are suitable for this stew.

Clean and bone the fish, then scald it and wipe well with a cloth. Heat the oil in a fireproof casserole and fry the fish, browning all over. Lower the heat and leave it to cook very gently until it is tender. Take it out of the casserole and put it aside, but keep it warm.

In the same casserole, using the same oil, sauté the onion, garlic and parsley. Add the tomato purée, stir in the vinegar, and then pour in about 600ml (1 pint) of boiling water. Cook very slowly for 30 minutes. Return the fish to the pan and simmer until the fish is thoroughly reheated.

Serve very hot with croutons.

Italian cooking

Fish
I Pesci

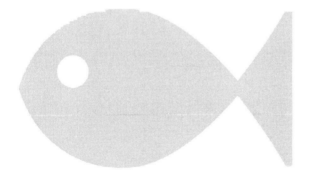

Italian cooking

Boiled Carp

Carpione in Umido

Although carp was at one time popular in this country, it seems to have gone completely out of favour. On the Continent, however, it is still greatly esteemed and often appears at Christmas Eve or on Holy days when meat is not allowed.

Put into a fish kettle or a large saucepan about 900ml (1½ pints) of red wine, you need enough to cover the fish, a sprig of fresh thyme, 2 bay leaves, a few thin slices of onion, salt and black pepper. Bring this mixture to the boil, then immediately reduce the heat.

Wash and clean about 700g (1½lb) of carp, scale it and then put it into the hot wine. Cover and cook very slowly for 30 minutes or until the fish is tender.

In a small saucepan make a white roux and dilute this with warmed red wine. Cook, stirring all the time, for at least 5 minutes, then pour the sauce into the pan in which the carp is cooking. Stir, until well-blended with the rest of the wine, and continue cooking for another 5 minutes. Remove the thyme and the bay leaves, and then serve the carp with the sauce poured over it and a good squeeze of lemon juice.

Stuffed Mackerel

Sgombro Ripieno

Carefully clean as many mackerel as you require, make a slit in the tummy of each and remove the centre bone without breaking the fish. It can be done, the art is to rub away at the back of the fish until the bone gradually loosens itself and comes away with comparative ease.

Fry lightly in olive oil some chopped onion, the same quantity of dried and chopped mushrooms, previously soaked, and a good handful of chopped fresh parsley. When the onions are soft mix them with enough white breadcrumbs to give the stuffing body. Add as much grated lemon rind, chopped fresh thyme and grated fresh Parmesan cheese as you like for flavouring. Work all this to a smooth paste and then pack it into the mackerel. Sew up the slits and then, with your fingers, press the fish back into its original shape. It should look as though it had not been touched.

Brush each fish with olive oil, then place them in a well-greased oven casserole. Bake at 190°C/375°F/Gas 5 for about 30 minutes, or until the fish is tender, basting fairly frequently.

Serve with thin slices of lemon and a cold potato salad.

Italian cooking

Salt Cod Croquettes

Crocchette di Baccala

450g (1lb) salt cod	Breadcrumbs
1 small onion, chopped	1 egg
2 tablespoons fresh parsley, chopped	Olive oil
125ml (4fl oz) thick cheese sauce	Black pepper

Soak the fish for 12 hours in cold water, changing the water 2 or 3 times. Wash it well, drain it, and put it into a pan with cold water. Bring to the boil and cook for 20 minutes. Strain, skin and shred the fish and mix with the onion and parsley. Pass everything through a mincer using the coarsest grater.

Beat the egg, stir in the sauce, add plenty of black pepper and then the minced cod and onions. Leave for 30 minutes in a cool place, then shape into croquettes. Roll in milk and breadcrumbs and fry in deep boiling oil until brown.

Serve hot, sprinkled generously with lemon juice. These cakes make a good breakfast dish and, oddly enough, are excellent with scrambled egg.

Salt Cod, Venetian Style

Baccala alla Veneziana

900g (2lb) salt cod	4 tablespoons olive oil
4 large onions, chopped	Black pepper
6 anchovies, shredded	Milk

Soak the cod for 12 hours, changing the water 2 or 3 times. Heat the oil in a saucepan, add the onion and brown it lightly. Then add the anchovies, sprinkle with pepper, and last of all add the cod well-drained and dried. Fry to a golden brown, then add enough milk to cover and simmer gently until the fish is tender and most of the milk is absorbed. Serve with mashed polenta (cornmeal).

Marinated Eel

Capitone Marinato

900g (2lb) eel
1 clove garlic, chopped
3 cloves
3 peppercorns
Salt and pepper

Plain flour
Olive oil for frying
300ml (1/2 pint) olive oil
300ml (1/2 pint) tarragon vinegar

Skin, bone and clean the eel. Cut it into 5cm (2in) lengths. Wash the pieces and dry them well with a cloth, then roll them in well-seasoned flour. Heat the oil and fry the eel pieces until they are browned. Arrange in a shallow dish and leave until they are cold.

Make a marinade in a saucepan with equal quantities of oil and vinegar. Add the garlic, peppercorns, a very little salt and the cloves. Bring all this to the boil, remove from the heat and leave until quite cold. Pour this over the eel and leave for another 12 hours.

Another method is to clean and wash the eel, dry it thoroughly and roll it in flour, previously well-seasoned. Arrange in a large casserole in the shape of a letter 'S'. Cover with the marinade and cook very gently for about 40 minutes, basting from time to time. Remove from the heat and leave for 12 hours or even longer. Serve cold.

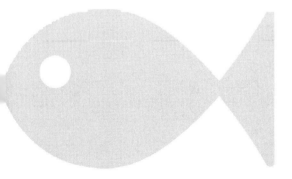

Italian cooking

Fricassee of Frogs' Legs

Rank in Fricassea

900g (2lb) frogs' legs
225ml (8fl oz) dry white wine
100g (4oz) small mushrooms
600ml (1 pint) chicken stock
1 onion, chopped
1 clove garlic, chopped
Butter for frying
Single cream

Salt and pepper
Milk
Lemon rind
Flour
Marsala
Bay leaves, fresh rosemary
  and fresh parsley

Usually frogs' legs are sold all ready for cooking. Wipe them with a damp cloth, dip in milk, rub with salt and pepper and lightly dust with flour.

Melt the butter, brown the onion, garlic, mushrooms and frogs' legs. Do not let them become more than a pale golden colour. Add the dry white wine, simmer for 5 minutes, add the stock, bay leaves, rosemary, salt, pepper and 2 strips of lemon rind and cook for 10 minutes, by which time the meat will be very tender. Remove the frogs' legs, put them aside and keep hot. Add to the pan 125ml (4fl oz) of Marsala and enough cream to thicken the sauce. Remove bay leaves, rosemary and lemon rind and pour the sauce over the frogs' legs. Serve well-sprinkled with fresh parsley, and garnished with triangles of fried bread.

Fried Frogs' Legs

Rank Fritte

Dip the frogs' legs in milk, rub in salt and pepper then coat thoroughly with batter. Dry in deep boiling oil and serve with slices of lemon.

Or just dust the frogs' legs with flour and dip in beaten egg before frying. Serve with tomato sauce, or wedges of lemon.

Red Mullet baked in Parchment

Triglie nella 'Papillote'

Red Mullet	Olive oil
Dried mushrooms	Greaseproof paper or foil
Fresh parsley	Salt and black pepper
Bacon	Lemon juice
Garlic	

The quantity of ingredients for this recipe naturally depends on the number of fish used.

Soak the mushrooms in tepid water for 30 minutes. Wash them well and chop them in small pieces. Chop the bacon, parsley and garlic, and then lightly fry all these ingredients in hot oil.

Clean the fish but do not remove the liver, as this is a delicacy.

Cut the paper into heart-shaped pieces. On each piece spread a layer of the mushroom and bacon mixture, then add 1 fish and spread this with some more of the mixture. Season with salt and black pepper, add a squeeze of lemon juice, then fold the paper firmly round the fish. Bake at 230°C/450°F/Gas 8 for 15 to 20 minutes. Serve in the paper.

Baked Grey Mullet

Cefali al Forno

Clean the mullet and score on either side. Rub with salt and pepper. Brush an oven casserole with oil, and sprinkle it well with chopped fresh parsley and lemon juice before putting in the fish. Bake at 150°C/300°F/Gas 2 until tender.

Serve with boiled potatoes, preferably new, tossed in butter and chopped fresh parsley.

Italian cooking

Red or Rock Mullet, Leghorn Style

Triglie alla Livornese

6 mullet	Fresh thyme
1 onion, chopped	Bay leaves
1 stick celery, chopped	Salt and pepper
900g (2lb) tomatoes, chopped	Plain flour
Fresh parsley	Olive oil for frying

Clean the mullet, season them and roll them in flour. Heat the oil and fry the onion, celery and parsley. When these are brown, add the tomatoes, thyme and bay leaves, and simmer until they are very soft. Pass through a sieve and return to the pan.

In another pan lightly brown the mullet in hot oil, and then transfer them to the tomato sauce. Simmer them gently until they are tender.

Serve the mullet in the sauce, garnished with fresh parsley.

If you do not care for fish fried in oil, the mullet can be simply simmered in the sauce without previous browning.

Mussels Fried in Oil

Muscoli Fritti nell'Olio

Clean, wash and prepare the mussels as in the following recipe to the point of removing the black weed. Drop each mussel into a bowl of good frying batter and then fry in boiling hot olive oil. Drain off the surplus fat on absorbent paper and knock off odd bits of batter, these are apt to adhere and give the flavour of 'all batter and no mussel' unless one is careful.

Sprinkle with lemon juice and serve very hot, either as an appetizer with drinks or in a dish of *fritto misto*.

Mussels cooked in Tomato Sauce, Tuscany Style

Muscoli alla Toscana

2.3 litres (4 pints) mussels
1 onion
Fresh thyme and parsley

Salt and pepper
150ml (¹/4 pint) dry white wine
150ml (¹/4 pint) water

Sauce

450g (1lb) peeled and chopped
  tomatoes

Oil or butter for frying

Scrape and brush the mussels and wash them in several waters until all the grit is removed. Put into a large pan the wine, water, onion, thyme, a handful of parsley, salt, pepper and the mussels. Cover and cook rapidly, shaking the pan at frequent intervals. As soon as the mussels open they are cooked. Remove them from the pan with a perforated spoon, take them from their shells and remove the beard. Discard any that do not open.

Heat the butter or oil in a pan, add the tomatoes and simmer until these are soft. Stir to a pulp, add the mussels and simmer gently for 2 minutes, not a second more or the mussels will harden. Serve the mussels in the tomato sauce with triangles of bread crisply fried and smeared very lightly with crushed garlic.

Italian cooking

Fried Oysters

Ostriche Fritte

This is a recipe for which one can well recommend bottled or tinned oysters, or even mussels.

Heat about 24 oysters in their own liquid, then drain (reserving liquid) and chop very finely.

Put into a small saucepan 150ml (1/4 pint) of fresh single cream and the same quantity of oyster liquid. Thicken with flour, stir and cook for 3 minutes. Add the same quantity of butter as you have of flour and continue simmering gently. Remove from the heat and cool. Beat the yolks of 2 eggs and whisk swiftly into the sauce. Return to the heat, add the chopped oysters, stir vigorously and cook for 1 minute. Remove finally from the heat, add 6 stoned and finely chopped black olives and flavour with salt and pepper. Leave for several hours or until the mixture is very cold. Break off small pieces, form into balls, dip these in a frying batter and then fry in deep boiling oil until brown. Serve with any suitable fish sauce garnished with fresh sprigs of parsley and thin slices of lemon. It is not difficult to prepare oysters in this manner and the result is an interesting and delicious appetizer.

Fried Scampi

Scampi Fritti

Scampi Fritti is a favourite dish of the Venetians, and if you should find yourself within the region of the canals you should certainly order yourself a dish of them. Today in Britain scampi has become the fashionable name for salt-water crustaceans like Dublin Bay prawns (*langoustine*), whether they are true scampi or not.

Take the flesh from the shells of as many scampi or prawns as you require, dip them in a good frying batter and fry them quickly in a pan of deep boiling oil until they are crisp. Pile on a dish, garnish with fresh parsley and thin slices of lemon, and serve piping hot.

Snails, Roman Style

Lumache alla Romana

Once a year on the Feast of San Giovanni the people of Rome like to eat snails. With them they drink fairly large quantities of good white wine. The following method of preparing snails is strictly Roman: it takes considerable time, but if you are fond of snails it is probably well worthwhile.

1.4 kg (3lb) snails	1 fresh sprig mint
Vinegar and plain flour	2 hot peppers
8 anchovies	150ml (¼ pint) olive oil
4 cloves garlic	Salt and pepper
4 large tomatoes	4 slices bread

Stir into the snails (with your hands) a mixture of coarse salt, plain flour and vinegar until the snails are completely covered with foam. Repeat several times until there is no more foam. Wash the snails under running water until quite free of the flour and salt, and then put them into a pan with water to cover and leave them there for 5 minutes and drain well.

Fill another pan with cold water, put the snails into this and cook them over a low heat until they begin to show their heads. At once increase the heat and cook rapidly for 10 minutes. Strain, and once more drop them into cold water. Using another pan, heat the oil, add the garlic, the anchovies, tomatoes, and enough of the snail liquor to make a sauce. Simmer for 15 minutes. Add the mint and the peppers and simmer for another 5 minutes. Drop in the snails and continue simmering for another 45 minutes. Remove the mint.

Serve the snails in their sauce, and leave it to those who eat them to remove them from their shells. Do not forget to serve some white Italian wine with them, it is an essential part of the meal.

Italian cooking

Marinated Fried Sole

Sogliola in 'Saor'

The Venetians eat this dish on the Feast of the Redemption, 19 July.

2 large soles
3 onions, chopped
25g (1oz) raisins
25g (1oz) plain flour
25g (1oz) pine nuts

300ml (1/2 pint) wine vinegar
Cinnamon
3 tablespoons olive oil
Salt and pepper

Wash and skin the fish, remove the heads and the fins but do not fillet. Mix the flour with the seasoning and rub this well into the fish.

   Heat the oil and fry the onions until brown, then remove them from the heat but keep them hot. Put the fish, the nuts and the raisins into the same pan and fry the fish on both sides until it is a deep golden brown. Remove with care and place in a deep dish. Return the onions to the pan, add the vinegar and bring to the boil. Take this sauce from the heat, leave it until cold and then pour it over the fish, completely covering it. Leave it for several hours before serving cold.

Grilled Swordfish

Pesce Spada alla Graticola

The flesh of the swordfish is rather dry but both the texture and the flavour are good. This recipe is typical not only of Italy but of much of the Mediterranean.

700g (1½lb) swordfish
Juice 1 lemon
2 tablespoons olive oil

1 tablespoon chopped fresh parsley
Salt and pepper

Skin the fish and cut it into cubes about 3.5cm (1½ in) square.

Prepare a marinade by blending the oil and lemon, salt, pepper and parsley, and leave the fish in this for 1 hour, turning from time to time to ensure that the marinade is well-absorbed.

Place the fish under a grill, about 10cm (4in) from the heat, and cook for 5 minutes. Remove from the heat, brush with the marinade, and return once more to the grill, this time browning the other side.

If grilling is difficult, roll the marinated fish cubes in beaten egg and well-seasoned breadcrumbs and fry them in deep boiling oil until brown.

Serve with slices of lemon and fresh sprigs of parsley.

Halibut may be prepared in the same manner.

Whitebait Fritters

Frittelle di Bianchetti

These fritters are served with *fritto misto*.

Wash and clean the whitebait and drain on a sieve. Make a thick frying batter. Drop the fish first into this and then quickly into a pan of boiling hot oil. Do not put too many in at the same time otherwise they may stick to each other.

Serve with crisply fried parsley and thick slices of lemon.

Italian cooking

Trout with Anchovy Sauce

Trote in Salsa D'acciughe

450g (1lb) small trout
25g (1oz) butter
6 anchovies
1 tablespoon mixed chopped
  fresh parsley and mint

Salt and flour
Lemon juice and a little grated
  rind
150ml (1/4 pint) Marsala
Olive oil

Wash the fish well and dry thoroughly. Trim, but do not scale. Rub with a little salt and roll in flour. Fry in very hot olive oil until brown. Arrange the fish on a serving place but keep them hot.

In another pan melt the butter, add the anchovies, then the wine. Stir and simmer for 5 minutes. Just before removing from the heat stir in the parsley and the mint, they must both be very finely chopped, and add a few drops of lemon juice and 1/2 teaspoon of grated lemon rind. Pour this sauce over the trout and serve immediately.

When cooking trout in oil, use only the very best grade.

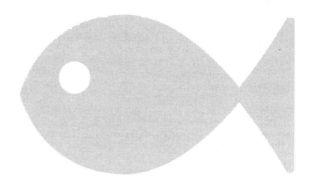

Trout in White Wine

Trote in Bianco

900g (2lb) small trout
600ml (1 pint) dry white wine
1 carrot, chopped
1 stick celery, chopped
1 onion
1 tablespoon olive oil

Rind and juice 1 lemon
600ml (1 pint) water
2 fresh sprigs parsley
1 bay leaf
Salt and pepper

Prepare the trout as in previous recipe. Heat the oil in a deep pan and lightly brown the trout. Remove them from the pan and put on one side to keep hot. In the same pan brown the vegetables and add the wine, water, lemon juice and the lemon rind cut into strips (but with the pith removed), the parsley, the bay leaf, salt and pepper. Return the trout to the pan and simmer it gently until it is tender.

Remove the trout, arrange on a serving dish and keep it warm while you pass the remaining ingredients (except for bay leaf and lemon rind) through a sieve. Pour some of the sauce over the trout, and serve the rest separately.

If trout is not available, try cooking other small fish in this manner.

Italian cooking

Grilled Tuna Fish

Tonno alla Graticola

In Italy, tuna fish is considered a delicacy. Its white flesh is not unlike veal in texture and has an excellent flavour.

The best part of the tuna for grilling is the belly cut into thick steaks.

Make a marinade with olive oil, thinly sliced onions, 1 or 2 bay leaves, salt and pepper, and a little lemon juice. Leave the fish in this for about 2 hours, then grill each steak on both sides for 7 minutes.

Serve very hot with a garlic and anchovy sauce, which it is advisable to make before cooking the steaks.

Anchovy Sauce

Crush 2 cloves of garlic with 4 to 5 chopped anchovies and a handful of chopped fresh parsley. Add just enough olive oil, drop by drop, to make a smooth paste. Dilute with a few drops of lemon juice, and as soon as the steaks are grilled pour the sauce over them and serve at once.

Poached Whiting

Nasello in Umido

700g (1 1/2lb) small whiting or
  haddock
2 cloves garlic, chopped
1 onion, chopped
1 carrot, chopped
1 stick celery, chopped

450g (1lb) tomatoes, chopped
2 fresh sprigs parsley, chopped
Fresh basil
2 tablespoons olive oil
Salt and pepper
50g (2oz) tomato purée

Clean the fish and score them on one side but leave them whole.

Heat the oil in a large pan; brown the garlic and all the vegetables except the tomatoes. Add the fish, parsley, a little basil, salt and pepper and lastly the tomatoes. Simmer for 15 minutes. Dilute the tomato purée with enough fish stock or water to cover the fish. Pour this into the pan and cook everything gently until the fish is tender. Serve the fish and the vegetables together.

Baked Fish in Parchment

Pesce nella 'Papillote'

This recipe for which you will need greaseproof paper or foil can be used with almost any type of white fish.

6 fillets, not too thick
75g (3oz) mushrooms, chopped
1 large onion, chopped
200g (7oz) crabmeat or the same
  quantity of fresh crab
1 egg (beaten)

Butter or oil for frying
Dry white wine
300ml (1/2 pint) fish stock
Salt and pepper
Plain flour

Almost any type of white fish can be used for this recipe.

Clean the fillets, rub them with salt and pepper and sprinkle them with lemon juice. Heat some butter or oil in a frying pan and fry the fillets until they are a golden brown. Remove from the pan and keep warm. Put the crabmeat into the same pan, stir in the egg, add some salt and pepper and 125ml (4fl oz) of wine. Simmer over a low heat stirring all the while, until the egg and wine mixture thickens. Put aside, but keep this warm, too.

In another pan fry the onion with the mushrooms, dredge both with flour and stir and cook for 2 to 3 minutes. Pour in some white wine to flavour, and then gradually add the fish stock, previously heated.

Cut and grease some squares of greaseproof paper. Place a fillet of fish on each, spread it with a layer of crabmeat, then cover with another fillet. Pour some sauce over the whole. Carefully fold up the paper so that nothing can escape and bake at 230°C/450°F/Gas 8 for 15 minutes. Serve in the paper.

Italian cooking

Whiting Cooked in Wine

Stufato di Nasello Fresco

About 4 small whiting
300ml (1/2 pint) dry white wine
1 onion, chopped
1 carrot, chopped
1 stick celery, chopped

1 fresh sprig parsley, chopped
Salt
Black pepper
1 bay leaf
1 tablespoon olive oil

Trim and wash the fish and score on one side only. Rub with salt and black pepper.

Heat the oil in a deep pan, lightly fry the vegetables and the parsley, then pour in the wine. Bring quickly to the boil, add the bay leaf and the fish, then reduce the heat and cook the fish slowly until it is tender, about 10 minutes should be enough but it does depend on the size of the whiting.

Take the fish from the pan, arrange on a serving dish and keep warm. Put the wine and the vegetables through a sieve, reheat and serve this sauce poured over the fish.

Fish Stewed in Vegetable Sauce

Pesce col Salsa

900g (2lb) whiting or small
  haddock
1 large onion, chopped
1 large carrot, chopped
2 sticks celery, chopped
4 tomatoes, chopped
A little butter or oil
Several bacon rinds

2 cloves garlic, chopped
Fresh basil
Plain flour
Milk
Salt and pepper
Nutmeg
Grated fresh Parmesan
  cheese

Clean the fish, remove the heads and tails, but otherwise leave whole. Heat the oil and butter together, fry the bacon rinds until crisp and then remove them, add the garlic, onion, carrot and celery, and when these are browned, the tomatoes. Simmer for 20 minutes or until all the vegetables are soft. Pass through a sieve. Return to the pan, and thicken with enough boiling milk and a little flour to make a sauce in which gently to stew the fish. Add the fish, salt and pepper and a good pinch of nutmeg and chopped fresh basil, and cook until the fish is tender.

Serve the fish in the sauce, sprinkled with grated Parmesan cheese, and accompanied by buttered noodles or plain boiled potatoes.

Italian cooking

Fish in Casserole

Pesce in Casseruola

900g (2lb) filleted white fish
2 carrots, sliced
2 sticks celery, sliced
700g (1¹/2lb) tomatoes, sliced
1 large onion, sliced
25g (1oz) almonds

1 large fresh sprig parsley, chopped
50g (2oz) dried mushrooms, chopped
Fish stock (optional)
Salt and pepper
Fresh marjoram
Butter or oil

This is one of the best ways that I know of dealing with those plain uninteresting looking slabs of haddock or cod fillets. If you have no fish stock, then use dry white wine and water instead. Tinned button mushrooms can take the place of dried when the latter are not available.

Blanch and lightly fry the almonds. Grease an oven casserole, and cover the bottom with the tomatoes. Add half the mushrooms, the carrots and celery. Season with plenty of salt and pepper, and pour in enough liquid to cover. Add the fish, then the remaining mushrooms, the onion, parsley and almonds. Bake at 190°C/375°F/Gas 5 for about 30 minutes or until the fish is tender.

If you prepare this fish casserole in the morning, it is better, for by the time you need it the flavour of the various ingredients has penetrated into the fish.

Stuffed Fish

Pesce Farcito

1 large fish
2 fresh sprigs parsley, chopped
100g (4oz) soft breadcrumbs
2 rashers of streaky bacon
150ml (1/4 pint) dry white wine

1 large onion, chopped
Salt and pepper
150ml (1/4 pint) milk
Olive oil and butter for frying
1 lemon

Carp, large trout, etc. are all suitable for this recipe.

Thoroughly clean and prepare the fish but do not remove the head.

Chop the bacon and mix it with the onion, parsley, breadcrumbs, salt, pepper and roe, if any, and when thoroughly mixed moisten with a good squeeze of lemon juice. Lightly fry this mixture in butter then pack it tightly into the fish. Sew up the side of the fish firmly or fix with small skewers, and brush it with olive oil.

Grease a large oven casserole, dredge it with breadcrumbs, and dot the fish with thin slivers of butter. Put it in the casserole, and sprinkle it with breadcrumbs. Pour in the wine and bake for 10 minutes at 190°C/375°F/Gas 5. Add the milk and continue baking until the fish is tender, basting frequently to prevent it drying.

Italian cooking

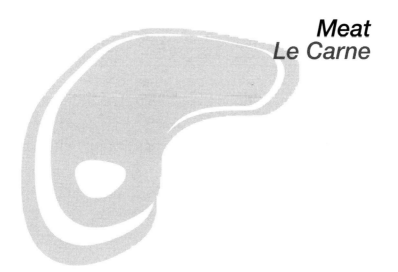

Meat
Le Carne

Ham Cooked with Marsala

Prosciutto Cotto al Marsala

Naturally the best type of ham to use for this recipe is the Italian prosciutto with its tangy flavour. Failing this, thick slices of very lean gammon bacon or ham make a good substitute.

Make a roux and dilute it with enough Marsala to make a fairly thin sauce in which to cook the bacon. Simmer the slices in this sauce for about 15 minutes. Add a very little salt and pepper.

Tinned sweet cherries with some of their juice, added just before the bacon is ready, give the dish that delightful sweet-sour flavour so appreciated by the Italians.

Braised Beef, Italian Style

Bue Braciato

Grease and rub with garlic, a good-sized round of beef, such as topside. Sprinkle it with salt and pepper and flavour it with fresh thyme and rosemary. Heat in a braising pan 2 tablespoons of olive oil 25g (1oz) of butter. Brown the meat all over, then add 2 thickly sliced onions, 2 carrots sliced lengthways and 1 stick of celery broken into 2.5cm (1in) lengths. Brown the vegetables, add a handful of chopped fresh parsley, 1 to 2 thin strips of lemon rind and 100g (4oz) of tomato purée previously diluted with 225ml (8fl oz) of water, and a 600ml (1 pint) of burgundy.

Cook very slowly for about 4 hours, by which time the sauce will have become thick, and the meat so tender that it almost falls apart at the touch. Slice the meat, strain the vegetables and gravy through a sieve. Pour this over the meat before serving.

Italian cooking

Spiced and Boiled Beef

Rondello di Manzo

Rub a piece of beef, such as topside, weighing 1.4kg (3lb), with garlic, salt and pepper. Make a marinade by bringing 600ml (1 pint) of red wine, a teaspoon of vinegar, 1 sliced onion, 1 sliced carrot, a chopped stick of celery, a few peppercorns and 3 cloves almost to the boil. Leave to cool, then pour this marinade over the beef. Leave for 24 hours, turning the meat about three times. Remove the meat from the marinade, dry it thoroughly with a cloth and strain the marinade. Using a braising pan, brown the beef in butter, pour over it the marinade, cover the pan tightly and simmer until the meat is tender, basting occasionally.

Roast Beef, Italian Style

Manzo Arrosto

Rub a joint of beef, such as topside, with garlic, salt and pepper, and cover with strips of streaky bacon. Place it in a baking tin, with plenty of chopped onion and enough fresh rosemary to flavour. Roast at 190°C/375°F/Gas 5. Baste occasionally with warm red wine and bake slowly until the meat is tender.

Beef Braised in Wine

Bue Stufato al Vino Rosso

Rub about 900g (2lb) of stewing steak with salt, pepper and grated nutmeg. Place in a bowl, cover with vin rose, though ordinary red wine will do if the other is not at hand, and add 2 bay leaves and a clove of chopped garlic. Leave for 3 hours, then dry the meat thoroughly and strain the wine.

Heat some olive oil in a saucepan and fry 3 to 4 bacon rinds, removing them as soon as they are crisp, and brown 1 chopped onion. Dust the meat with flour, brown, and then add the strained wine marinade. Cover and cook very slowly until the meat is tender. If necessary add either boiling beef stock or water during cooking if the meat appears to be dry.

Beef Stewed in Wine

Carne in Umido

900g (2lb) stewing beef	*Fresh marjoram or fennel seeds*
50g (2oz) streaky bacon	*2 cloves*
1 onion	*Butter and oil*
1 carrot	*4 tomatoes, peeled and sliced*
1 stick celery	*Dry white wine*
2 cloves garlic, chopped	*Plain flour*
Handful chopped fresh parsley	*Salt and pepper*

Hammer the beef lightly, cut it into cubes and roll in flour. Clean, peel and chop all vegetables.

Heat the oil then fry the bacon until crisp. Remove from the pan, and brown the onion, carrot and celery. Add the meat, garlic, cloves, parsley and marjoram or fennel. Cook fairly quickly until the meat is well browned. Add the tomatoes, simmer for 5 minutes, then pour in the wine, of which there must be enough completely to cover the meat and the vegetables. Cook gently until the meat is tender. Serve either with plain boiled potatoes or rice.

Italian cooking

Beef 'Hats'

Cima alla Genovese

450g (1 lb) thinly sliced steak
50g (2oz) chopped minced pork
50g (2oz) breadcrumbs
50g (2oz) grated fresh
  Parmesan cheese
450g (1 lb) cooked green peas
2 cloves garlic, chopped
1 carrot, chopped

1 stick celery, chopped
1 onion, chopped
Salt and pepper
Fresh marjoram
Red wine
Single cream or plain flour
Lemon juice

Lightly pound the steak, taking care not to tear it. Each slice needs to be large enough to hold 1 teaspoon of stuffing, therefore each piece should be roughly 5 x 7.5cm (2 x 3in) in size.

Stuffing

Mix the pork, breadcrumbs, cheese, peas, marjoram, salt and pepper together to make a stuffing. Moisten with some beef stock or water. Put a teaspoon of this mixture on to each slice of meat. Fold the meat round the stuffing and mould into hatlike shapes (or balls, if the hats defeat you). Sew them up with a needle or tie with cotton to keep firm. Place the rolls in a pan large enough to take them all flat on the bottom and just cover with boiling water. Add the chopped carrot, onion, celery and garlic and cook very gently until the rolls are tender.

Take out the rolls. Rub the vegetables and gravy through a sieve and return to the pan. Add a little red wine to the sauce, thicken with cream or flour. Reheat the rolls in this sauce and serve.

Beef Steaks, Neapolitan Style

Costa di Manzo alla Pizzaiola

450g (1lb) steak fillets
450g (1lb) sliced onions
450g (1lb) sliced tomatoes
2 cloves garlic, chopped
Fresh oregano or marjoram

Salt and pepper
Oil for frying
2 tablespoons single cream
Plain flour

Lightly beat each fillet, rub with salt and pepper, dredge with flour and then sauté in hot oil until brown on both sides. Remove them from the pan but keep hot.

In the same oil fry the onions, garlic and tomatoes until brown but not soft. Return the steaks to the pan, add a good sprinkling of either oregano or marjoram and leave the meat to simmer gently in the vegetables until it is tender and has absorbed their flavour.

Stir in the cream and serve the steaks in the sauce.

Steak, Hunter's Style

Bistecca alla Cacciatora

Wipe the required number of beef steaks with a damp cloth and dip them in well-seasoned plain flour. Heat some oil and butter together and flavour it with garlic and 1 finely chopped onion.

Brown the steaks on both sides then cover them with peeled and sliced tomatoes. Simmer them for 5 minutes, then add salt, pepper, chopped fresh parsley and a pinch of fennel seed. Continue to cook slowly until the meat is tender. Add 150ml (1/4 pint) of Marsala or red wine a few minutes before serving.

Italian cooking

Lamb, Hunter's Style

Abbachio alla Cacciatora

Wipe about 900g (2lb) of loin or breast of lamb with a damp cloth. Cut into serving portions and rub with salt, pepper and garlic.

Heat in a braising pan enough olive oil to brown the meat. Add a fresh sprig of rosemary, a little fresh sage, a whole clove of chopped garlic and 1 tablespoon of plain flour. Stir all these ingredients together then add 225ml (8fl oz) of dry white wine and 125ml (4fl oz) of wine vinegar. Cook fairly quickly until the sauce is thick, then add 225ml (8fl oz) of hot lamb stock, cover the pan and simmer the meat until tender. About 30 minutes should be enough. Baste from time to time and add more hot water if necessary to prevent drying. Just before the meat is ready, add 4 to 5 anchovies to the sauce.

The meat should be so tender that it is almost falling off the bone, and should be served in the sauce.

If desired, add some lamb's kidneys, as they do in Rome.

Lamb Marinated and Fried

Agnello Fritto

Wipe a leg of lamb with a damp cloth, rub it with lemon, salt and pepper. Put it into a pan and, using as little water as possible, simmer it very gently until tender. Remove from the pan, leave until cold enough to slice evenly.

Rub a bowl with garlic and lay the slices of mutton in it. Combine an equal quantity of water and tarragon vinegar to make a marinade, enough to cover the meat, adding a little black pepper, 2 to 3 cloves, a piece of mace, about 2 tablespoons of olive oil and 2 bay leaves. Heat the marinade almost to boiling point, allow it to cool, then pour it over the meat. Leave for 24 hours.

Dry the meat, dip in beaten egg, roll in breadcrumbs and fry in deep boiling oil. Strain the marinade and thicken it with flour. Simmer a full 10 minutes.

Serve the thickened marinade separately. Garnish the meat with slices of lemon and fresh watercress.

Parmesan Cutlets

Costolette alla Parmigiana

450g (1lb) lamb (or veal) cutlets
2 eggs
50g (2oz) grated fresh Parmesan
  cheese

50g (2oz) breadcrumbs
Mozzarella cheese
Salt and pepper
Olive oil for frying

Rub the cutlets with salt and pepper and leave them for 30 minutes. Beat the eggs. Combine the breadcrumbs and grated Parmesan cheese. Dip the cutlets into the beaten egg, then thoroughly coat them with the mixed cheese and breadcrumbs. Do this twice. Thinly slice the mozzarella.

Heat the olive oil and brown the cutlets lightly on both sides. As each cutlet is ready, place it in a shallow casserole and cover each with a thin slice of mozzarella cheese. Spread with a thin layer of tomato sauce and bake at 190°C/375°F/Gas 5 until the cheese has browned. This takes about 15 minutes.

Serve very hot with young green peas and potato purée.

Failing mozzarella cheese, use any soft cheese that will slice thinly and can be cooked.

Milk Lamb Cutlets in Tomato Sauce

Bracioline D'Agnello al Pomidoro

Milk lamb cutlets are rare in Britain but often lamb or veal cutlets can be cooked in this way provided that they are very tender.

Rub lightly with salt and pepper about 8 cutlets, then brown them on both sides in hot butter. Pour over them 150ml (1/4 pint) of dry white wine and simmer them gently until the wine has evaporated, then add 2 tablespoons of tomato purée diluted with 150ml (1/4 pint) of water.

Continue to simmer, very gently indeed, until the cutlets are tender and have absorbed most of the tomato sauce. Serve either with chopped spinach, or French beans and slices of lightly fried tomatoes.

Italian cooking

Mock Steaks with Anchovies

Bistecche 'Hachees'

700g (1¹/2lb) stewing steak
6 mashed anchovies
2 beaten eggs
Plain flour
Breadcrumbs
A little butter or oil

225ml (8fl oz) red wine
Fresh sage
Plain flour or single cream
Pepper
Parsley butter

Put the meat through a mincer and mix it with the anchovies. Add pepper, but no salt for the anchovies are sufficiently salty, and bind with 1 egg. Knead and shape into steaks. Roll them in flour, the remaining egg, and very fine breadcrumbs.

Heat the oil and butter together, add the sage and lightly brown the steaks on both sides. Pour in the wine fairly slowly and continue cooking until it has evaporated. Add a little boiling water and simmer until the 'steaks' are quite cooked through, turning them over once during cooking.

Remove from the pan and place on each 'steak' a pat of parsley butter and 1 to 2 thin strips of anchovy. Thicken the gravy with either a little flour or cream and serve separately.

Meat Balls, Florentine Style

Polpettine alla Fiorentina

275g (10oz) minced beef
50g (2oz) minced bacon
50g (2oz) grated fresh Parmesan
 cheese
1 beaten egg
3 tablespoons brown
 breadcrumbs

1 onion, chopped
1 stick celery, chopped
1 carrot, chopped
Salt, pepper and nutmeg
Beef stock
Butter or oil for frying
Plain flour

Mince the meat, bacon and onion together twice. Heat a little butter or oil, fry the meat for 5 minutes then add 600ml (1 pint) of beef stock and simmer gently until the meat is cooked through. Remove it from the stove and when it is cool add the egg, breadcrumbs, cheese, salt, pepper and nutmeg. Mix everything to a paste, then shape it into balls. Roll in flour.

Heat a little more butter or oil, brown the celery and carrot and then the meat balls. Pour in enough stock to almost cover and simmer gently for 30 minutes. Take the balls from the pan with a perforated spoon and keep them warm in a serving dish. Put the vegetables and stock through a sieve, and pour this gravy over the meat balls.

Italian cooking

Meat Balls on Skewers

Spiedini

450g (1lb) minced beef or lamb
2 beaten eggs
50g (2oz) grated fresh Parmesan
  cheese
100g (4oz) breadcrumbs
2 tablespoons chopped fresh
  parsley

1 clove garlic, chopped
Salt and pepper
Bacon cut into squares
Bread cut into cubes
Oil for frying

Combine the meat, parsley, cheese, breadcrumbs, garlic, salt and pepper and pass once through a mincer. Bind with the eggs. Shape into 'bullets' and leave for 30 minutes in a refrigerator.

Thread the *spiedini* on to skewers with a cube of bread and a piece of bacon between each *spiedini* and the next. Fry in deep boiling fat and serve on the skewers with a plain rice risotto.

The *spiedini* can also be grilled. Brush them with olive oil and place at least 10cm (4in) below the heat. Grill for about 15 minutes, turning several times.

Roast Lamb in Anchovy Sauce

Abbacchio in Salsa D'acciughe

Wipe a leg of lamb with a damp cloth. Make several gashes in the flesh with a sharp knife and insert into these slivers of garlic. Rub the meat with salt, pepper and a little ground ginger. Place on the trivet in a roasting pan and bake at 190°C/375°F/Gas 5 until tender. Baste first with warm dry white wine, then with hot lamb stock or water.

Remove the meat, and mix with the gravy 3 to 4 fresh anchovies, a handful of finely chopped fresh parsley and a teaspoon of grated lemon rind.

Stir all these ingredients together, bring to the boil, thicken slightly with plain flour, cook for 5 minutes, then serve meat and sauce separately.

Roasted Suckling Lamb

Agnellino al Forno

Both young lamb and kid are prepared as an Easter speciality in Italy. Occasionally in London's Italian shops one is able to buy a whole kid, and of course a lamb. The same recipe, however, does for both. Kid, when properly prepared, is very good. If not available use two large leg joints.

1 lamb, about 3.6kg (8lb)	Single cream or plain flour
450g (1lb) cooking apples	Streaky bacon
6 cloves garlic, sliced	Lemon juice and peel
Cloves	Oil or butter
Salt, pepper and ginger powder	

Rub the prepared lamb (or kid) inside and out with lemon juice and peel. Core the apples, wrap them in strips of bacon, and push a clove into each. Put these in or around the lamb. With a sharp knife make slits on either side of the lamb and insert slivers of garlic. Rub it with a mixture of salt, pepper and ginger, and brush with hot oil or butter.

Roast until tender at 190°C/375°F/Gas 5, allowing about 15 minutes for every 450g (2lb), and basting every 15 minutes with boiling water or hot apple juice. Remove from the pan and thicken the gravy with cream or flour and pass it through a sieve.

Fried Liver

Fegato Fritto alla Salvia

Thinly slice the liver and leave it to soak for 1 hour in milk. Drain, dry thoroughly, then roll it in plain flour flavoured with pepper.

Heat a little butter and flavour it with fresh sage. Very slowly fry the liver until tender, shaking the pan from time to time to prevent burning.

Remove the liver. Add enough plain flour to the butter to make a roux, then thin to a sauce with red wine. Stir the sauce well, strain and pour over the liver before serving.

Italian cooking

Braised Liver, Trieste Style

Fegato alla Triestina

450g (1lb) liver
1 tablespoon breadcrumbs
1 onion, chopped
1 carrot, chopped
1 stick celery, chopped
225g (8oz) sliced tomatoes

1 clove garlic
Handful chopped fresh parsley
Pepper, fresh sage and cloves
Lemon
125ml (4fl oz) olive oil for frying
Fried bread

Scald the liver for 5 minutes in boiling water. Drain it, and cut it into slices. Stick 1 clove into each slice. Heat the oil, and fry the breadcrumbs, onion, carrot and celery until a light brown.

Arrange the liver on top of the vegetables. Add the tomatoes, pepper, sage and garlic and just cover with cold water. Cover, bring once to the boil, then simmer until the liver is tender. Remove the liver from the pan, remove cloves, and arrange it in the middle of a serving dish surrounded by fingers of crisply fried bread.

Rub the gravy and vegetables through a sieve and pour this over the bread. Add a good squeeze of lemon and garnish with parsley.

Liver and Onions

Fegato alla Veneziana

350g (12oz) calves' liver
2 large onions, chopped
1 tablespoon chopped fresh
  parsley
150ml (1/4 pint) red wine

Plain flour
Paprika
Black pepper
50g (2oz) butter

This simple dish is claimed by the Venetians as their invention, and it has, whatever its origin, become a national and international dish.

Wash the liver in cold water, dry it thoroughly and cut it into slices. Roll it in flour seasoned with black pepper and paprika.

Heat the butter and brown the onions. Add the liver, lightly brown it on both sides, then add the wine. Simmer for 5 minutes, add the parsley and continue to simmer gently until the liver is tender.

Pork Cutlets Marinated and Grilled

Costolette di Maiale Marinate

Rub a mixing bowl with garlic and make a marinade with about 150ml (1/4 pint) of tarragon vinegar, the same quantity of dry white wine and 2 tablespoons of olive oil. Flavour with salt, chopped fresh parsley, a clove, nutmeg, a small onion and black pepper. Whip up well and leave the cutlets in it for 2 hours.

Take the cutlets from the marinade and grill them on both sides until tender. Serve with a hot caper sauce.

Italian cooking

Mortadella Fritters

Costolette di Mortadella

Dip as many thick slices of mortadella as required in a thick coating of batter to which some béchamel sauce has been added. Fry in deep boiling fat until a golden brown.

Tipsy Pork

Maiale Ubriaco

Rub as many pork chops as required with lemon, salt and pepper. Grease a pan and heat it well before adding the chops. Brown on both sides over a low heat, then add red Chianti or another type of red wine. Simmer gently until the chops are tender, turning them at least once. Much of the wine will have been absorbed during the cooking, but what is left should be poured over the chops when serving.

Roast Pork with Prune Sauce

Lombatine di Maiale con Salsa di Prugne

Score a loin of pork and rub with lemon juice, garlic, salt and pepper. Put it into a roasting pan, with a little rosemary, the juice of 1 lemon and 225ml (8fl oz) of boiling water. Roast at 190°C/375°F/Gas 5, basting fairly often. Just before the pork is ready baste it with 150ml (1/4 pint) of dry white wine and continue to bake until the wine has evaporated. Serve with a prune sauce (page 214).

Braised Ox-Tongue

Lingua di Bue Braciata

1 tongue
6 anchovies
1 tablespoon capers
1 clove garlic, chopped
1 carrot, chopped
1 gherkin, chopped
Fresh parsley and basil

300ml (1/2 pint) dry white wine
1 tablespoon single cream
Streaky bacon
Bacon rinds
Salt and pepper
A little oil and butter

Soak the tongue for 1 hour in salted water. Drain and trim it, then boil it rapidly until you can remove the skin with ease. Cover with streaky bacon and put pieces of anchovy in between the bacon.

Heat the oil with the butter and fry the bacon rinds until crisp. Remove bacon rinds, brown the carrot, garlic, a good handful of parsley and some basil. Add the tongue, brown it, then pour in the wine. Simmer for a few minutes then add enough boiling water to cover. Add salt and pepper and one more tablespoon of oil. Simmer gently for about 4 hours, or until the tongue is tender.

Remove the tongue from the pan, and keep it warm. Rub the gravy and the vegetables through a sieve. Return to the pan, add the gherkin, the capers and a tablespoon of single cream. Simmer and stir to a smooth sauce. Serve the tongue together with the sauce.

Italian cooking

Tongue with a Sour-Sweet Sauce

Lingua di Bue in Salsa Agrodolce

Make a white roux, add salt and pepper and enough red wine and stock to make a sauce. Add 2 tablespoons of brown sugar, 1 tablespoon of pine nuts and 1 tablespoon of raisins and a heaped tablespoon of grated orange peel. Simmer these ingredients for about 15 minutes. Add as much sliced cooked tongue as required, pour 125ml (4fl oz) of sherry and continue to cook gently for another 10 minutes.

Serve the tongue in the sauce and garnish with watercress.

Tripe, Milan Style

Busecca (Trippa alla Milanese)

1.4kg (3lb) tripe	225g (8oz) fresh broad beans
2 onions	3 tablespoons tomato purée
3 leeks	Grated fresh Parmesan cheese
4 tomatoes	4 bacon rinds
2 sticks celery	Saffron and nutmeg
2 carrots	Salt and pepper
450g (1lb) potatoes	Butter and oil
1/2 small cabbage	3 cloves
Chopped fresh parsley	Slices of bread

Wash and scrape the tripe. Cut into serving pieces, cover with cold water, bring to the boil and cook for 5 minutes. Drain, throw away the water, cover once more, this time with boiling water. Add 1 stick of celery and 1 onion stuck with cloves. Bring to the boil and continue to cook over a moderate heat for 2 hours. Take out the tripe, thoroughly dry it, then if desired, marinate it in a vinegar and oil dressing for several hours. Strain the stock and reserve for later use.

Clean and slice or chop remaining vegetables. Fry the bacon rinds in equal parts of oil and butter, then brown the beans, carrots, leeks, the remaining onion and the celery. Add the tomatoes, simmer for 15 minutes, then add the tripe, salt, pepper, saffron and nutmeg. Simmer for a further 5 minutes, add the strained stock, potatoes, cabbage, tomato purée and parsley. Continue to cook slowly until everything is tender.

Then stir in plenty of grated Parmesan cheese. Serve in a tureen with fingers of bread, rubbed with garlic and fried in oil, floating on top.

Ragout of Veal

Osso Buco

This is one of the great dishes of Milan and is always served with rice, usually *risotto milanese*. There are two main points in the preparation of this dish, its flavouring, the *gremolata*, and the precious marrow from the bones. In most Italian homes and restaurants a small marrow fork is offered with which to dig out this delicacy which is usually spread on chunks of bread.

6 veal shin bones or veal shanks	*100g (4oz) butter*
6 large tomatoes	*225ml (8fl oz) red wine*
Salt and pepper	*1 clove garlic, chopped*
Plain flour	*2 tablespoons chopped fresh parsley*

The bones should each be about 7.5cm (3in) long and with some meat attached. Many butchers will correctly chop the bones for this dish if asked. Peel, seed and chop the tomatoes. Sprinkle the bones with salt, pepper and dredge lightly with flour. Heat the butter in a large saucepan, add the bones and brown them all over. Stand the bones in the pan so that they are upright and the marrow cannot fall out. Add the wine, cook for 10 minutes, then add the tomatoes. Cover the pan tightly and simmer until the meat on the bones is so tender it almost falls off. About 1½ hours should be sufficient.

Mix the remaining ingredients to make the *gremolata* and sprinkle over the bones 3 minutes before serving.

To present osso buco in the classical fashion, serve it surrounded by the risotto and with a dressing of melted butter and grated fresh Parmesan cheese.

Italian cooking

Veal 'Birds'

Vitello All'Ucceletto

Only the very tenderest of veal fillets are suitable for this.

Heat a little butter and oil together, add garlic and 1 bay leaf. As this begins to brown, fry the fillets on both sides, sprinkling them with salt and pepper as they cook. As soon as they are browned, place them on a serving plate. Remove the garlic and bay leaf from the pan and pour the fat drop by drop on to the meat. Serve at once.

The flavour and virtue of this dish depends entirely on the quality of the veal and the accompanying ingredients, i.e., the butter and oil, and the speed with which the veal appears on the table after it has been cooked.

Another way to prepare veal 'birds' is to cut the fillets into cubes and push these on to a skewer with a piece of bacon between each cube. Sprinkle with salt, pepper and chopped fresh rosemary, then grill under a good heat. They need no other accompaniment than the fat and meat juice which falls into the grill pan.

Veal Rolls a la Rossini

Involtini di Vitello alla Rossini

450g (1lb) veal
75g (3oz) chopped bacon
1 tablespoon chopped fresh
  parsley
3 slices white bread
75g (3oz) grated fresh Parmesan
  cheese
1 clove garlic, sliced

Lemon juice
1 small onion, sliced
Butter for frying
Fresh sage or rosemary
Several cubes white bread
Oil for frying
Salt and pepper
Beaten egg and breadcrumbs

Slice the veal thinly, then cut into 7.5cm (3in) squares. Lightly pound until the squares are very thin but try to keep their shape.

Soak the slices of bread in milk and squeeze them dry. Lightly fry the bacon in butter adding the onion and garlic. Combine with the soaked bread, cheese, parsley, salt and pepper. Knead to a paste and place a teaspoon of the mixture in the middle of each slice of veal. Roll firmly and secure each roll either with cotton or with toothpicks.

Dip each roll in lemon juice, beaten egg and breadcrumbs. Fix on long skewers, alternating with cubes of bread. Sprinkle with chopped fresh sage or rosemary and fry in deep hot oil until browned all over.

Serve very hot on the skewers.

Another method is to ignore the stuffing and spread each veal slice with anchovy paste and crushed capers.

Veal with Tuna Fish and Anchovies

Vitello Tonnato

900g (2lb) lean veal	3 cloves
8 anchovies	Juice 1 lemon
150g (5oz) tinned tuna fish	Dry white wine
2 egg yolks	Olive oil
1 carrot, chopped	Capers
1 stick celery, chopped	Salt and pepper
2 bay leaves	

Soak the veal for 30 minutes in cold water, dry it well and put it into a saucepan with a very small quantity of water. Add the vegetables, lemon juice, cloves, bay leaves, salt and pepper and 90ml (3fl oz) of dry white wine. Bring once to the boil then cook slowly until the veal is tender. Remove the meat, leave it to cool and continue to cook the liquid until it is reduced by half. Strain.

Mash the tuna fish with the anchovies, then rub both through a very fine sieve. Beat the egg yolks with a wooden spoon, add to them, drop by drop, enough olive oil to make a fairly fluid dressing. Blend in the veal gravy, add the fish and whisk until the dressing is smooth. Lastly add a few chopped capers.

Slice the meat, spread each slice with the dressing and arrange in a casserole. Cover and leave for several hours in a cool place before serving.

Garnish with thin slices of lemon and chopped fresh parsley.

Italian cooking

Veal Fillets with Ham

Saltimbocca

A recipe which, while it finds its origin in Brescia, is so popular in Rome that it has become a Roman speciality. For 4 people you need 8 thin slices of veal and the same amount of ham. Lightly hammer the veal, rub with lemon, salt and pepper and on each slice put a leaf of fresh sage. Cover with a slice of ham or gammon bacon. Fix with a toothpick and fry in oil or butter as quickly as possible.

Serve with artichokes, young peas, tiny Brussels sprouts or new potatoes.

Liver, Tuscan Style

Fegato alla Toscana

This is simply calves' liver, sliced horizontally, seasoned with black pepper, flavoured with fresh sage, and fried in deep hot oil.

Veal Fillets with Egg Sauce

Bistecchine di Vitello alla Zabaione

This is rather extravagant, a little exotic, but very good.

6 veal fillets	2 beaten egg yolks
6 slices bread	150ml (1/4 pint) Marsala
Salt, pepper and sugar	Butter for frying
Lemon juice	

First make the sauce. Season the eggs and add just one tablespoon of sugar, then whip in the wine and 1 tablespoon of boiling water. Put this mixture into the top of a double boiler and cook it slowly, stirring all the time, until it is thick. Put aside, but keep it warm.

Trim the veal fillets until each is exactly the same shape and size. Very lightly hammer each and rub with lemon juice, salt and pepper. Sauté in butter, browning on both sides. Fry the bread, each slice should be the same shape but a little larger than the veal fillets.

Put one veal fillet on each slice of bread, cover with the egg sauce (*zabaione*) and serve immediately.

Veal with Marsala

Scaloppine al Marsala

Flatten as many veal fillets as required and rub with lemon juice. Dust with seasoned plain flour and brown quickly on both sides in butter. Add 150ml (1/4 pint) of Marsala and continue to cook very slowly until the meat is tender.

Serve garnished with fresh watercress and slices of lemon.

Italian cooking

Poultry and Game
I Polli

Chicken Aretina

Pollo all'Aretina

2 plump young chickens
2 chopped onions
300ml (1/2 pint) dry white wine
600ml (1 pint) chicken stock

Olive oil for frying
225g (8oz) shelled garden peas
100g (4oz) long-grain rice
Salt and pepper

Joint the cleaned chickens into suitable serving pieces, and rub each with salt and pepper. Heat the olive oil in a pan, lightly fry the onions, and just as these begin to change colour add the chicken pieces. Brown these well, pour in the wine, simmer for 5 minutes, then add the stock. Bring once to the boil, add the rice and the peas, salt and pepper. Cook over a moderate heat for 20 minutes.

Serve everything together.

Chicken Baked in Cream

Pollo alla Crema

Joint a plump and clean young chicken, about 900g (2lb) into serving pieces. Lightly rub with lemon and then roll in seasoned plain flour. Heat a fairly large piece of butter in an oven casserole and brown the chicken pieces on top of the stove. Pour in enough fresh single cream to cover the chicken completely, and then bake the chicken at 190°C/375°F/Gas 5 until tender, basting from time to time with the cream.

Remove the chicken from the casserole and keep warm. Thicken the cream with the thinnest possible potato flour and water paste, add 225ml (8fl oz) more of cream, a good flavouring of brandy and bring all just to the point of boiling. Serve the chicken in the sauce.

One way to serve chicken cooked in cream is to make a rice ring and to serve the chicken in the centre with the sauce poured over it. This is a delicious dish but cannot be made with substitutes, it's butter and cream or nothing.

Italian cooking

Chicken Marsala

Pollo Marsala

Joint a young chicken, rub it well in seasoned plain flour, then brown it either in olive oil or butter. Add enough Marsala to cover, and simmer gently until tender. Serve in the sauce.

Chicken Maddalena

Pollo alla Maddalena

1 chicken, about 1.4kg (3lb)
1 onion, sliced
2 cloves garlic, sliced
1 tablespoon chopped fresh
* parsley*
1 stick chopped celery
150ml (1/4 pint) brandy

Boiling chicken stock
12 black olives
4 anchovies
1 bay leaf
125ml (4fl oz) olive oil
* for frying*
Salt and pepper

Joint a cleaned chicken into serving pieces. Rub with salt, pepper and the bay leaf.

Heat the oil and fry the onion, celery, garlic and parsley to a light brown. Add the chicken joints and fry these until golden. Pour in the cognac, simmer until this has evaporated and then add enough boiling stock to cover. Continue to cook slowly until the chicken is tender, then add the olives, stoned and chopped, and, just before serving, the anchovies.

Chicken, Hunter's Style

Pollo alla Cacciatora

1 or 2 chickens, each about
  900g (2lb)
1 large onion, chopped
2 cloves garlic, left whole
4 tomatoes, peeled and sliced
300ml (1/2 pint) dry white wine

2 tablespoons chopped
  fresh parsley
1 rasher of bacon, diced
Salt and pepper
Hot chicken stock
125ml (4fl oz) olive oil

Joint the chickens and rub them with salt and pepper. Heat the oil, lightly fry the onion, add the chicken pieces, and when these are a golden brown, add the garlic and the wine and simmer for about 10 minutes. Add the tomatoes, bacon and parsley, simmer for another 10 minutes or so, remove the garlic, and then almost cover the chicken with boiling stock. Cook slowly until the chicken is tender.

Italian cooking

Chicken, Neapolitan Style

Pollo alla Napoletana

1 boiling fowl, about 1.4kg (3lb)
100g (4oz) dried mushrooms
2 cloves garlic, sliced
2 tablespoons tomato purée
2 large onions, chopped

25g (1oz) Italian bacon or ham
300ml (1/2 pint) dry white wine
Fresh rosemary
25ml (4fl oz) olive oil
Salt and pepper

Rub the bird with salt and pepper, put it into a pan with plenty of salted water, cover well and cook slowly until it is tender, about 2 to 3 hours, depending on the age of the bird.

The mushrooms may be chopped or left whole; soak then for 30 minutes in tepid water. Dice the bacon.

Heat the oil in a pan and fry the onions until they begin to change colour, then add the mushrooms, bacon, garlic and rosemary. Simmer gently until the onions are soft, stir in the tomato purée and 2 tablespoons of the chicken stock. Continue to simmer for another 10 minutes, then add the wine.

Take the chicken from the pan and joint it. Place the pieces in the sauce and leave them to simmer until they have absorbed some of its flavour. Serve the chicken in the sauce.

This is an excellent way to deal with tough birds, the sauce gives it flavour and from the boiling you have a pot of stock for making soup.

Chicken Spatchcock

Pollo alla Diavola

This very simple but usually successful method of grilling chickens belongs to Tuscany, and the chicken is eaten traditionally at the Feast of the Impruneta, accompanied by a bottle or two of good Chianti wine. It needs very young and plump chickens, and without these there is no point in attempting it.

Split open from the back as many young chickens as required. Spread out and flatten, use a heavy iron, and rub with lemon juice. Fix them with skewers to keep them flat and lay them in a marinade of olive oil, chopped fresh parsley, onion, ground ginger and plenty of salt and pepper. Leave them there for several hours, for one of the secrets of this dish is the subtle flavour of ginger. Place the chickens under a hot grill and brown on both sides. Remove the skewers, garnish the chickens with slices of lemon, and serve with a fresh watercress salad.

I need hardly say that the flavour of these chickens is even better when they are grilled over a charcoal fire.

Pigeons, provided that they are tender, may be prepared in the same way. Serve with a sauce.

Italian cooking

Chicken, Roman Style

Pollo alla Romana

1 chicken, about 1.4kg
  (3lb)
150ml (¼ pint) dry white wine
1 clove garlic, sliced
50g (2oz) tomato purée

Fresh rosemary
2 rashers bacon
125ml (4fl oz) olive oil
Chicken stock
Salt and pepper

Joint the chicken, rub the pieces with salt and pepper and then brush with olive oil. Dice the bacon. Heat the oil in a deep pan, add the bacon, the garlic and then the chicken pieces, and fry until they are a golden brown. Sprinkle them with chopped rosemary, salt and pepper, pour in the wine and simmer for several minutes. Add the tomato purée and enough hot stock to make a sauce. Cook slowly until the chicken pieces are tender, and serve in the sauce.

Chicken Stew

Pollo in Umido

1 large boiling fowl, about 1.8kg
  (4lb)
2 large onions, chopped
2 green peppers, chopped
6 peeled tomatoes, chopped
1 teaspoon sugar

450g (1lb) shelled garden peas
50g (2oz) dried mushrooms
12 green olives
225ml (8fl oz) olive oil
Plain flour for thickening
Salt and pepper

Joint the fowl into serving portions. Rub the pieces with salt and pepper and then with flour. Heat the oil and brown the chicken pieces. Remove them and keep them hot. In the same oil fry the onions, peppers, olives and tomatoes for about 15 minutes. Add the sugar then replace the chicken pieces and pour in sufficient hot water to cover. Cook slowly, tightly covered, until the chicken pieces are almost tender. Add the peas, the mushrooms, previously soaked and chopped, and a thin flour and water paste. Cover the pan again and continue to cook gently until the peas are soft.

You can also add long-grain rice to this stew at the same time as you add the peas. A good pinch of saffron adds a different and distinctive flavour, but this should not be added until the chicken has been cooking for about 1 hour.

Braised Duck with Lentils

Anitra con Lenticchie

1 duck, about 1.4–1.8kg (3–4lb)
150–300ml (¹/4–¹/2 pint) Marsala
1 onion, chopped
1 carrot, chopped
1 stick celery, chopped
2 rashers bacon, chopped
6 stoned green olives

125ml (4fl oz) olive oil
Fresh chopped parsley and thyme
Dessert apples
Salt and pepper
2 bay leaves
Lentils
Chicken stock

Truss the duck loosely as for roasting and rub inside and out with salt and bay leaves. Stuff with cored but *not* peeled dessert apples.

Heat the olive oil in a large braising pan. Fry the bacon; onion, carrot and celery and then the duck, turning it so that it browns all over. Pour the Marsala over it and simmer until the wine evaporates. Add the parsley, thyme and olives and enough stock or water to cover the bottom of the pan, and simmer gently until the duck is tender. Baste from time to time.

Cook the lentils in the usual manner, adding a little chopped garlic and celery. Mash to a purée, adding some of the gravy from the duck.

Remove the duck, scoop out the stuffing, this can be used as a garnish, rub the gravy and vegetables through a sieve, and serve separately as a sauce. Serve the duck surrounded by mashed lentils and the apples.

Italian cooking

Duck with Noodles

Pappardelle coll'Anitra

This dish, for which I think a rather ancient duck is adequate, is eaten in Florence on 10 August, the Feast Day of St Lorenzo.

1 duck, about 1.4–1.8kg (3–4lb)	*Salt and pepper*
450g (1lb) tomatoes	*Butter or oil*
300ml (1/2 pint) red wine	*Wide noodles*
Fresh sage and rosemary	*1 teaspoon sugar*

Joint a prepared duck and rub it well with salt. Peel and chop the tomatoes and simmer them gently in butter or oil until they are soft. Add sugar, salt, pepper, sage and rosemary. Stir altogether and when the tomatoes are sufficiently soft, add the pieces of duck. Pour in the wine and simmer gently until the duck is tender. During cooking add, if necessary, either some more wine or hot chicken stock to prevent burning. Strip the meat from the duck pieces and chop very finely. Return the meat to the pan and cook for another 10 minutes.

Cook the noodles in plenty of boiling, salted water until they are tender. The time depends on the size and the quality of the noodles, but they should not take more than 20 minutes. Drain well, then stir them into the duck and serve immediately.

Wild Duck

Anitra Selvatica

1 wild duck	Salt and pepper
Chopped fresh parsley	Oil and butter
Juice and rind 1 orange	Dessert apple or celery
150–300ml (1/4–1/2 pint) Marsala	1/2 clove garlic, chopped

The flavour and treatment of wild duck depends much on the time of year and the duck's local feeding habits. If the flavour is mild, then it needs merely to be wiped with a damp cloth. If it is strong, then it should be well-washed and stuffed with dessert apple or celery, either of which will absorb the duck's strong flavour. This stuffing should be removed before serving the duck. If a wild duck is not available, a farmed one will do.

Heat some oil and butter in a roasting pan and place the duck, well brushed with olive oil, in the pan breast down. Bake at 190°C/375°F/Gas 5 until tender, allowing about 40 minutes per kg (20 minutes per lb). Baste from time to time with a Marsala basting sauce. Duck, like wild goose, should not be overcooked as its flesh becomes dry and crumbly.

Basting Sauce

Heat in a small saucepan about 2 tablespoons of olive oil, add the parsley, garlic, salt and pepper and, when very hot, the Marsala. Bring this quickly to the boil so that it will blend more easily, then add the orange juice and rind. Baste the duck with this fairly often and when the duck is cooked add, if liked, a little fresh single cream and some more Marsala to the sauce and serve separately.

Italian cooking

Game Birds Cooked in Marsala

Beccafichi al Marsala

Intended for all kinds of small game birds

12 small game birds
12 stoned black olives
Olive oil for browning
2 cloves garlic, chopped
150ml (1/4 pint) Marsala
4 peppercorns
50g (2oz) tomato purée

8 anchovies
6 tablespoons chicken stock
1 juniper berry, crushed
150ml (1/4 pint) dry white wine
Slices of bread
Salt and pepper

Clean the birds and rub them with salt and pepper and a crushed juniper berry. Heat the olive oil and brown the birds, then remove them from the pan, but keep them warm. Dilute the tomato purée with the stock and gradually pour this into the pan in which you have browned the birds. Stir until the oil and the tomato stock are well-blended, add the garlic, peppercorns, olives and anchovies and stir everything together before adding the white wine. Simmer for 1 to 2 minutes, then return the birds to the pan. Cover and cook very slowly until they are tender. Just before serving add the Marsala.

Fry until very crisp some slices of bread, 1 slice should do for 2 birds if the latter are very small. Place the birds on the bread, pour the sauce over birds and bread and serve immediately.

Hare in Sour-Sweet Sauce

Lepre in Agrodolce

1 hare, or rabbit
600ml (1 pint) red wine
1 onion, chopped
1 carrot, chopped
1 stick celery, chopped
3 juniper berries
2 bay leaves
3 cloves
1/4 stick cinnamon
3 large sliced onions

2 tablespoons olive oil
25g (1oz) butter
25g (1oz) plain flour
Salt and black pepper
25g (1oz) chocolate powder
225ml (8fl oz) double cream
2 tablespoons sugar
2 tablespoons raisins
1 tablespoon pine nuts

Joint the hare or rabbit, taking care not to break its bones. Add the wine, the onion, carrot, celery, juniper berries, cloves, bay leaves and cinnamon. Put the pieces of hare or rabbit into this mixture. See that they are well-covered and then leave for 24 hours.

Next day heat the oil and butter, and fry the sliced onions until soft but not brown. Dredge with flour, stir this well into the onions and cook gently for another 5 minutes. Remove the hare or rabbit from the marinade and add it to the onions. Take the cinnamon from the marinade, then pour the rest into the pan with the hare or rabbit. Season very generously with salt and black pepper and add 1 heaped tablespoon of powdered chocolate, *not* cocoa, and stir this well into the sauce. Add the sugar, pine nuts and raisins and continue to cook over a very moderate heat for another 30 minutes. Add cream, reheat but do not boil.

Other furred game can be cooked in this kind of sauce. Although at first glance the combination of chocolate and onions may seem startling it is not so. The taste of the chocolate is drowned by the many other flavours, and it serves more to darken the sauce than anything else.

Casserole of Pheasant

Fagiano in Casseruola

1 pheasant
Butter
Salt and pepper
50g (2oz) raisins
300ml (1/2 pint) brandy

300ml (1/2 pint) dry white wine
150ml (1/4 pint) Madeira
Pinch ground clove
1 juniper berry, crushed

Rub the pheasant inside and out with salt, brush with olive oil and a little crushed juniper. Put it into a casserole with plenty of butter and brown, using the top of the stove. Pour in the cognac, cover the pan and put it into the oven. Baste from time to time.

While the pheasant is cooking make the following sauce. Simmer the raisins in enough hot water to cover, until plump. Drain thoroughly and put them into a small saucepan with about 25g (1oz) of butter. Add the wines, seasoning and ground clove. Simmer very gently for 5 minutes. When the pheasant has been cooking for about 30 minutes, baste it with this sauce. Continue to cook the pheasant in the sauce, basting at least twice before cooking time is over. The average pheasant takes about 45 minutes to cook in a covered casserole.

Serve the pheasant in the sauce and with chestnut purée.

Casserole of Pigeons

Piccoine Selvatico all'Uso Umbro

This recipe is intended for wood pigeons and they can be simmered in a casserole for just as long as it takes to make them tender.

In an ordinary frying pan heat enough oil to fry the required number of pigeons, add salt and pepper and the juice of 1 whole lemon to 2 to 3 pigeons. Prepare the pigeons as for roasting but leave the heads on and the giblets intact. Fry until brown. In a fireproof casserole heat a little more olive oil, add some slices of bacon, the quantity depends on your personal taste, salt, pepper, some chopped fresh sage and then the pigeons. Pour the oil in which they have been browning over them and then add 300ml (1/2 pint) of dry white wine. Simmer until the wine has been reduced, then add enough hot stock to cover completely the bottom of the casserole. Add more stock during cooking if necessary.

When tender, remove the pigeons from the casserole, chop off the heads, take out the giblets and joint the pigeons. Add 1 to 2 anchovies, some chopped fresh parsley, chopped capers and enough hot stock to turn all these ingredients into a sauce. Bring to the boil, then simmer for about 10 minutes. Rub everything through a sieve, return to the casserole, add the pigeon, reheat and serve hot. Serve with noodles, with rice or with well-creamed potatoes.

Italian cooking

Pigeon Ragout

Ragu di Piccione

2 or 3 pigeons
25g (1oz) bacon, chopped
1 carrot, chopped
1 large onion, chopped
1 stick celery, chopped
2 tablespoons fresh parsley,
  chopped
2 tablespoons dried mushrooms,
  chopped

225ml (8fl oz) Marsala
Salt and black pepper
50g (2oz) butter
2 tablespoons olive oil
Chicken stock or water
Single cream or plain flour

Joint the pigeons. Heat the butter and oil together in a braising pan and sauté the bacon, carrot, celery and onion. Add the pieces of pigeon, brown them all over, add parsley, salt and pepper, then cover with boiling stock or water. Throw in the mushrooms, previously soaked, and cook very slowly until the pigeons are tender. Pour in the Marsala and simmer for another 5 minutes.

Remove the pigeons and arrange them on a large serving dish. Keep them hot. Rub the gravy and vegetables through a sieve, return this to the pan, add either cream or a thin flour and water paste, reheat and then pour over the pigeons. Surround with long-grain rice and serve hot.

Roast Pigeons

Piccione Arrosto

Italian pigeons are much plumper and more succulent than their British relatives. Properly jointed an Italian pigeon can be made to feed 4.

Prepare the pigeons as you would roasting chickens, rubbing the breasts well with olive oil and covering them with strips of streaky bacon. Put into each pigeon a large piece of sage-flavoured butter: this helps to keep them moist. Put them in a roasting tin with plenty of hot butter or oil, season with salt and pepper and bake at 190°C/375°F/Gas 5, basting frequently, for about 30 minutes or until the pigeons are tender. Just before they are ready remove the bacon, baste again and leave them to brown. Avoid overcooking. Joint and serve on toast or well-fried bread.

If you prefer to serve the pigeons whole, stuff them first before roasting. Grated fresh Parmesan cheese, breadcrumbs, chopped onion, raisins and pine nuts all make a good stuffing for pigeons.

Wild pigeons are not very good for roasting as they are usually far too tough.

If you do not care for sage, parsley butter can take its place.

Italian cooking

Rabbit in a 'Frying Pan' Roman Style

Coniglio in Padella

The best type of pan for this recipe is thick-bottomed, not too deep and having a tightly fitting lid.

Clean and joint the rabbit and cut into convenient pieces for serving. Soak in cold water for several hours. Dry on a cloth and rub with salt, pepper and fresh savoury herbs.

Heat enough olive oil in the pan to sauté the rabbit pieces, add 1 clove of sliced garlic, 4 rashers of bacon, 1 heaped teaspoon of chopped fresh parsley and 150ml (1/4 pint) of dry white wine. Simmer until the wine has disappeared and then add 6 chopped and peeled tomatoes and enough hot stock or water to prevent burning and for basting. Cover firmly, and cook very slowly until the rabbit is tender, basting from time to time.

Serve the rabbit with its sauce, and with a platter of risotto.

Fried Rabbit

Coniglio Fritto

Only a very young rabbit is suitable for frying. Clean it well, joint it neatly, or get the butcher to do this for you, and soak the pieces in cold water for several hours. Dry each piece with a cloth, then rub with lemon juice, salt and pepper.

Dice several rashers of fatty bacon and fry in olive oil until very crisp. Add the rabbit pieces and brown lightly on both sides. Continue to fry gently until cooked through.

Serve very hot with a fresh watercress salad and thin slices of lemon garnished with redcurrant jelly.

The rabbit pieces may also be dipped in beaten egg and rolled in breadcrumbs before frying, or, if you are keen on batter, dip them first into a good coating batter and fry in deep, hot, bacon-flavoured olive oil.

Provided that the rabbit is tender it can be almost as good as chicken and is considerably cheaper.

Rabbit, Hunter's Style

Coniglio alla Cacciatora

Clean, wash and joint a rabbit then leave it to marinate in burgundy or some other red wine for several hours.

Heat some olive oil and butter, enough to fry the rabbit in a fireproof casserole, and lightly fry a chopped onion, 2 sliced cloves of garlic, and the rabbit pieces previously well-dried. Season with salt and pepper, add a little hot chicken stock and simmer for 40 minutes. Sprinkle with chopped fresh rosemary, and then pour in the wine in which you marinated the rabbit. Continue to cook very slowly until the rabbit is tender, and if it is necessary to add more liquid, let it be warmed dry white wine. Cover the casserole while cooking.

There are numerous recipes styled 'Hunter's'. This is a simple one. Some add vegetables, others plenty of tomatoes, others treble the amount of onions, while some prefer fresh sage to rosemary.

Italian cooking

Roast and Stuffed Rabbit

Coniglio Ripieno al Forno

1 large rabbit
Streaky bacon
2 carrots, chopped
2 onions, chopped
1 stick celery, chopped

1 teaspoon chopped fresh sage
Salt and pepper
Olive oil
Lemon juice
Vinegar

Stuffing

50g (2oz) veal
50g (2oz) beef or lamb
50g (2oz) dried mushrooms
50g (2oz) breadcrumbs

Single cream or milk
1 tablespoon chopped fresh parsley
Butter

Clean the rabbit and wash it thoroughly in a mixture of vinegar and cold water. Leave it soaking in very cold water for several hours. Soak the mushrooms in tepid water for about 20 minutes, then wash them well under running water. Chop finely.

For the filling, put the meat through a mincer, mix with the mushrooms and the parsley, and fry lightly in butter for 5 minutes. Put this mixture into a bowl, add the breadcrumbs, salt and pepper, moisten with cream or milk, then knead to a paste.

Dry the rabbit on a cloth and rub inside and out with a mixture of salt, pepper, sage and lemon juice. Fill the rabbit with the stuffing and sew it up or fix it firmly with skewers. Cover with the bacon and place it in a baking tin previously heated and well-oiled. Surround the rabbit with the chopped vegetables, and bake at 230°C/450°F/Gas 8 until the rabbit is browned, then reduce the heat and continue baking until the rabbit is tender, basting often with boiling water, or red wine and boiling water mixed.

Remove the rabbit from the pan, pass the gravy and the vegetables through a sieve. Put the sieved sauce into a saucepan, reheat, add a little boiling water or hot chicken stock, skim off any excess fat and stir in a little cream just before serving. Serve the rabbit and the sauce separately.

Rabbit, in a Sour-Sweet Sauce Sicilian Style

Coniglio Agrodolce

1 rabbit
1.2 litres (2 pints) burgundy
2 onions, chopped
2 sprigs fresh parsley
1 sprig fresh thyme
4 peppercorns
1 bay leaf
2 cloves

A little butter and oil
600ml (1 pint) chicken stock
Salt and pepper
Sugar
Red wine vinegar
1 tablespoon sultanas
1 tablespoon pine nuts

Joint the rabbit, clean it well and leave it for several hours marinating in the burgundy. Remove the rabbit, put the red wine into a saucepan. Add an onion, the cloves, parsley, thyme, peppercorns and bay leaf. Bring to the boil, and then pour this marinade over the rabbit pieces. Leave for 30 minutes.

Heat the butter and the oil in a fireproof casserole and lightly fry an onion and the rabbit pieces. Strain the marinade and, when the rabbit pieces are browned, pour the strained marinade into the pan and simmer until it has been considerably reduced. Gradually add the stock, some salt and pepper and continue to cook slowly until the rabbit is tender.

Take 2 to 3 tablespoons of the liquid from the still simmering rabbit and put this into a small saucepan. Add the sugar and cook until this has completely melted. Pour in 90ml (3fl oz) of good quality red wine vinegar and stir everything with a wooden spoon. Add the sultanas and pine nuts and simmer for another 5 minutes. Pour this sauce over the rabbit and stir it into the gravy. See that each piece of the rabbit has some of the sour-sweet sauce. Serve very hot.

Italian cooking

Rabbit Stewed in Wine

Coniglio in Umido

Cut a rabbit into pieces as for Fried Rabbit (page 132), and after washing them well leave the pieces to soak for several hours in cold water. Dry on a cloth, rub with salt, pepper and fresh sage. In a saucepan heat some olive oil, butter and bacon and then sauté the rabbit pieces. Add plenty of chopped onion, at least 450g (1lb) of tomatoes, 150ml (¼ pint) dry white wine, and simmer until the wine has evaporated. Nearly fill the pan with hot chicken stock or water, add salt and pepper and continue to cook slowly until the rabbit is very tender.

Remove the rabbit pieces from the pan and put them into a deep and hot serving dish. Thicken the stock with a thin flour and water paste and cook for another 5 minutes. Pour the vegetables and sauce over the rabbit and serve with potatoes which have been boiled and then tossed in butter and chopped fresh parsley.

Fillets of Turkey Breast

Filetti di Tacchino alla Modenese

Slice the breast into fillets, each very thin, dip in beaten egg and seasoned breadcrumbs and fry lightly in butter until a golden brown.

Grease an oven casserole, one of the kind that can be used at table. Arrange some thin slices of bacon at the bottom, and cover them with slices of Gruyère cheese and then the turkey fillets. Add another layer of bacon and cheese and bake at 230°C/450°F/Gas 8 until the cheese melts. Serve at once, garnished with fried peppers and other green vegetables.

Roast and Stuffed Turkey

Tacchino Ripieno alla Lombarda

Stuffed turkey is a great Italian favourite and it can be bought, not only at Christmas but on other Feast Days, trussed and stuffed ready for the oven. Here is a stuffing from Lombardy.

100g (4oz) beef or lamb
50g (2oz) veal or pork
100g (4oz) pork sausage
75g (3oz) prunes
175g (6oz) grated fresh
  Parmesan cheese
900g (2lb) chestnuts
2 eggs
1 turkey trussed and ready
  for stuffing

300ml (1/2 pint) dry white wine
Mace
Fresh rosemary and sage
Salt and pepper
Butter and oil
Several rashers of bacon
1 clove garlic
1 onion

Soak the prunes overnight, stone and chop. Cook the chestnuts until easily skinned, then reboil and cook again until soft. Beat the eggs, mince the meats and the sausage. Mix all these ingredients together, add salt and pepper and fry very lightly in a little olive oil. Put into a bowl, add the cheese and the eggs, mash everything and then add a little dry white wine.

Push the stuffing into the neck and the body of the turkey. Sew up all apertures carefully. Heat plenty of butter in a roasting pan, add the onion coarsely sliced, garlic, mace, rosemary, sage and several rashers of bacon. Place the turkey on top of these ingredients and roast it until brown at 230°C/450°F/Gas 8. Reduce the heat, baste once with the wine previously heated, and then continue to roast it in a more moderate oven (190°C/375°F/Gas 5) until it is tender, basting frequently with either boiling chicken stock or water. Take out the garlic after 20 minutes' roasting.

When the turkey is tender take it from the pan, pass the gravy through a fine wire sieve and thicken it with a little single cream or flour and water paste. Serve the turkey and the sauce separately and surround the turkey with boiled chestnuts.

Italian cooking

Quail Cooked in Wine

Quaglie al Vino Bianco

6 quail (snipe, woodcock or
  plover)
2 small onions, chopped
2 cloves garlic, chopped
1 bay leaf
6 peppercorns
2 cloves

600ml (1 pint) dry white wine
300ml (1/2 pint) double cream
Salt and black pepper
Butter or olive oil
Raisins
Pine nuts
Croutons

Clean, draw and truss the quails. Fill each with a few raisins previously soaked in hot water until plump, and pine nuts. Brush generously with melted butter as quail can be very dry if not properly treated.

Heat enough oil or butter in a fireproof casserole to brown the quail. Sauté the onions, add the garlic, peppercorns, cloves and then the quail. Brown all over, add salt and pepper, then pour in the wine. Cover and simmer gently for about 30 minutes, then put the quail on to a hot serving dish. Strain the gravy through a wire sieve, return it to the casserole to reheat, and then stir the cream into it. Pour the sauce over the quail and serve them at once with fried croutons.

Vegetables
Erbaggi e Legumi

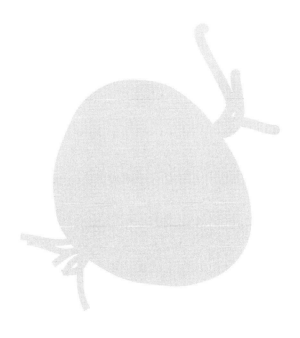

Italian cooking

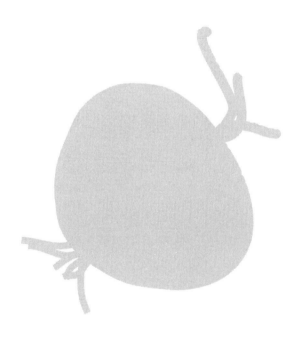

Fried Globe Artichokes

Carciofi alla Giudia

Much of the Roman cuisine is as seasonable as the weather. With the spring come the fresh, small artichokes and this way of cooking them is a Roman-Jewish speciality. Only very young artichokes can be used, as every part of the vegetable, including the choke, is eaten.

Wash the artichokes in salted water and drain, bottoms up. Trim the leaves to a point with sharp scissors and in between each leaf push some slivers of garlic. Fry in deep, boiling oil and, while the artichokes are cooking, sprinkle them with salt and pepper. Remove with a perforated spoon, drain free from oil, spread out the leaves slightly to give the artichoke the appearance of a flower, and serve with a vinegar dressing or melted butter.

Artichokes Cooked in Wine

Carciofi alla Romana

Use very small and fresh artichokes, wash them in salted water and drain, bottoms up. Trim the leaves to a point and push chopped fresh mint, parsley and salt well down between the leaves.

Heat a little olive oil and sauté the artichokes for a short while, then add dry white wine or strained chicken stock, 600ml (1 pint) of either to 12 artichokes. Continue to cook slowly until the artichokes are tender and most of the liquid has evaporated.

Serve cold and with the remaining liquid.

Asparagus Parmesan

Asparagi alla Parmigiana

450g (1lb) asparagus
50g (2oz) butter
Grated fresh Parmesan cheese

Salt, pepper and nutmeg
Lemon juice

Scrape the stalks of the asparagus, cut off any tough ends, these can be used in soup, and wash in cold water. Tie in bundles and place on the bottom of a large saucepan. Cover with boiling water flavoured with lemon juice. Cook fairly quickly until tender. Drain and arrange on a serving dish. Sprinkle with salt, pepper and nutmeg. Melt the butter and pour this over the asparagus, then sprinkle it with grated Parmesan cheese.

This recipe is suitable for both green or white asparagus and is, in fact, rather better with the thinner varieties.

Fried Asparagus

Asparagi Fritti

450g (1lb) cooked green
  asparagus
1 or 2 beaten eggs
Breadcrumbs

Salt and pepper
Fat or oil for frying
Flour

Tie the asparagus in bundles of 4 stalks. Dip in seasoned plain flour, then in beaten eggs and breadcrumbs. Fry in deep, boiling fat or oil until brown.

Baked Asparagus

Asparagi al Forno

Prepare asparagus as in preceding recipe but cook for 10 minutes only, using lemon-flavoured water. Place it in a well-greased baking dish, season it with salt and pepper, pour over it plenty of melted butter and cover all but the tips with grated cheese, preferably fresh Parmesan. Bake at 150°C/300°F/Gas 2 until tender, 20 minutes should be ample unless the asparagus is very tough. Sprinkle lightly with paprika before serving.

Fried Aubergine Slices

Melanzane Fritte

4 medium aubergines	Salt
Coating batter	

Wash the aubergines, cut off the stems, peel and slice thinly in rounds. Sprinkle the slices with salt and press between 2 plates. Leave for 1 hour. Wipe dry with a cloth and dip in coating batter. Fry in deep boiling fat until brown.

Alternatively you can dip the slices in egg and breadcrumbs, or fry *au naturel*. Serve hot.

Italian cooking

Aubergine Casserole with Cheese

Melanzane alla Romana

6 aubergines
225g (8oz) cottage cheese
50g (2oz) tomato purée

600ml (1 pint) stock
Olive oil for frying
Salt, pepper and mustard

Wash the aubergines, remove the stalks, peel and slice into thick rounds. Sprinkle with salt and press between 2 plates. Leave for 1 hour, wipe dry and fry *au naturel*. Arrange in layers in a greased oven casserole spreading cottage cheese between each layer. Thin the tomato purée with the stock, season with salt, pepper and mustard and pour this over the aubergine. Bake at 190°C/375°F/Gas 5 for 20 minutes.

Green Beans in Tomato Sauce

Fagiolini Verdi al Pomidoro

900g (2lb) green beans
1 tablespoon tomato purée
Salt and pepper
50g (2oz) butter

1 teaspoon sugar
Juice 1/2 lemon
1 grated onion

Wash the beans, and if they are very long break them into pieces. Cover with boiling water, add salt, and cook until tender. Drain well.

Melt the butter, lightly fry the onion, then add all the remaining ingredients, including the beans. Stir well so that each bean is well-coated with the sauce, and simmer gently for about 5 minutes before serving.

Broccoli Cooked in Wine

Broccoli al Vino Bianco

900g (2lb) broccoli or cauliflower
300ml (1/2 pint) dry white wine
1 clove garlic

Salt and pepper
125ml (4fl oz) olive oil

Cook the broccoli or cauliflower until almost tender. Drain and divide into flowerets.

Heat the oil, fry the garlic, remove it from the pan, add the flowerets and sauté to a golden brown. Add the wine and simmer until the flowerets are tender. Sprinkle with salt and pepper. Serve in the oil and wine sauce.

A Sicilian recipe similar to this includes stoned olives and uses *vin rosé* instead of white wine. Just before serving, 3 to 4 anchovies are added.

Fried Broccoli

Broccoli Fritti

900g (2lb) broccoli
1 or 2 beaten eggs
Plain flour

Oil for deep frying
Grated fresh Parmesan cheese
Salt and pepper

For this recipe one should use very firm green or mauve broccoli, with large heads.

Remove the green leaves, wash the broccoli and cook it in boiling salted water, with the heads clear of the liquid. Leave like this for 20 minutes then push the heads under the water and cook for another 10 minutes. Drain and season with salt and pepper. Divide into flowerets, roll these in flour and dip into beaten egg. Fry until a golden brown in deep boiling oil.

Serve generously sprinkled with grated fresh Parmesan cheese.

Cauliflower can be cooked in exactly the same way.

Italian cooking

Brussels Sprouts

Cavolini di Bruxelles

900g (2lb) Brussels sprouts
1 grated onion
50g (2oz) diced bacon

25g (1oz) butter
Salt
Grated fresh Parmesan cheese

Clean the sprouts, removing any wilted leaves, and soak them in cold water for 30 minutes. Wash well and cook in boiling, salted water until tender, but not soft. Drain very dry.

Melt the butter, fry the bacon and onion until brown, add the sprouts and toss them very gently in butter until a light amber colour. Serve with grated Parmesan cheese.

Or omit the bacon, onion and cheese, and instead add 225g (8oz) of whole cooked chestnuts to the Brussels sprouts while frying them in butter. Serve the sprouts and the chestnuts together.

Brussels Sprouts with Egg Sauce

Cavolini di Bruxelles in Salsa

450g (1lb) cooked Brussels sprouts
300ml (1/2 pint) vegetable stock
2 beaten eggs

3 tablespoons dry white wine
Salt and pepper
Butter

Melt the butter and slightly sauté the Brussels sprouts until they begin to change colour. In another pan warm the stock, season it and whisk the eggs into it. Simmer very gently until the mixture thickens. Take the sauce from the heat, whip it up, add the wine, whip again, then serve it poured over the sprouts. Ordinary runner or French beans are also excellent cooked in this way.

Cabbage Cooked in Wine

Cavoli al Vino Bianco

1 large white cabbage
1 grated onion
1 tablespoon capers
225ml (8fl oz) boiling water

225ml (8fl oz) dry white wine
Salt
1 teaspoon sugar
2 tablespoons olive oil

Wash the cabbage well, removing any wilted leaves, and cut it into quarters. Soak for 30 minutes in cold salted water. Thoroughly drain and shred.

Heat the oil in a saucepan, brown the onion, then toss the cabbage in the oil. Add water, salt and sugar and stir, then add the wine and capers. Stir everything together again, cover the pan and cook fairly slowly until the cabbage is tender, 15 minutes for a young cabbage and 25 for an older one should be enough. Drain the cabbage before serving, although there will not be much liquid.

Cauliflower with Lemon Sauce

Cavolfiore alla Villeroy

1 large cauliflower
2 beaten egg yolks
Juice 1/2 lemon

Salt and pepper
25g (1oz) plain flour
25g (1oz) butter

Remove the outer leaves and thick stalk of the cauliflower and soak it in salted water, head down, for 30 minutes. Rinse, cover with salted water and cook until tender. Drain (reserving liquid) and keep hot.

Make a roux with the butter and flour and thin it with 300ml (1/2 pint) of the cauliflower stock. Beat the eggs and lemon together until frothy. Take the white sauce from the heat, whip in the egg and lemon mixture, add seasonings, reheat, stirring all the time. Pour this sauce over the cauliflower before serving.

Italian cooking

Braised Fennel

Finocchi al Burro

700g (1 1/2lb) fennel
75g (3oz) butter

450ml (3/4 pint) vegetable stock
Salt and pepper

Wash and scrape the fennel and cut it into lengths. Simmer in butter until lightly browned. Add seasonings and stock and continue to cook gently until tender.

Another popular method of cooking fennel is to cook it slowly in stock until tender, then drain it well and arrange in a casserole. Sprinkle it generously with grated fresh Parmesan cheese, add salt and pepper and dredge lightly with fine breadcrumbs. Bake at 230°C/450°F/Gas 8 until the cheese has formed a thin crust.

Fennel is not unlike celery in appearance. It has thick fleshy leaves, and a crisp white bulb or root. Its flavour is vaguely that of aniseed, and is greatly appreciated in Italy. Although an acquired taste, it is generally liked by those who try it once or twice.

Mushrooms with Cheese

Funghi alla Parmigiana

Peel, wash and trim as many mushrooms as required. They should be fairly large. Place them, gills up, in a greased baking dish and sprinkle over them white bread crumbs, grated fresh Parmesan cheese, chopped fresh parsley and just the smallest amount of chopped garlic. Season with salt and pepper, pour a little boiling water in the bottom of the pan, top each mushroom with a small piece of butter or brush with olive oil and bake at 190°C/375°F/Gas 5 for 15 to 20 minutes.

Stuffed Mushrooms

Funghi Ripieni

450g (1lb) large mushrooms
1/2 clove garlic, chopped
1 onion, chopped
2 tablespoons fresh parsley,
  chopped
175g (6oz) minced beef or lamb

50g (2oz) soft breadcrumbs
1 tablespoon tomato purée
Few strips bacon
100g (4oz) butter
Salt and pepper

Wash the mushrooms and remove the stems. Melt the butter and gently simmer the mushrooms for 5 minutes. Remove the mushrooms from the pan, leaving the butter, and put them into a greased casserole.

Brown the meat and onion in the mushroom butter then add all the other ingredients except the bacon. Simmer for a few minutes then pile this mixture into the mushrooms. Cover each with a strip of bacon and bake at 190°C/375°F/Gas 5 for 20 minutes.

Sour-Sweet Carrots

Carote in Salsa Agrodolce

900g (2lb) carrots
2 tablespoons sugar
Salt and pepper
50g (2oz) butter

40g (1 1/2oz) plain flour
Carrot stock
3 tablespoons vinegar

Scrape or peel the carrots and slice either in rounds or lengthways. Cook in boiling, salted water in a covered saucepan until tender. Do not use more water than is necessary. Drain and reserve the liquid.

Melt the butter, add the flour and stir to a roux. Add salt and pepper, then enough of the carrot stock to make a sauce. Add sugar and vinegar and continue to simmer gently until the sauce is thick and smooth. Stir the carrots into the sauce, simmering until they are thoroughly reheated.

Italian cooking

Leeks au Gratin

'Flan' di Porri

900g (2lb) leeks
2 rashers bacon
225ml (8fl oz) single cream or
  milk
1 or 2 beaten eggs

Salt, pepper and nutmeg
25g (1oz) plain flour
Grated fresh Parmesan cheese
2 tablespoons olive oil

Wash and trim the leeks, leaving as much of the green part as possible.
Cook in boiling salted water until tender.

Heat the oil, dice and fry the bacon. Sprinkle with flour, add the cream
and cook until the sauce is smooth. Add salt, pepper and nutmeg. Take from
the heat and beat in the egg(s).

Drain the leeks and turn them into a greased oven casserole. Pour the
sauce over them, sprinkle generously with the grated cheese and bake until
the cheese has browned.

Stuffed Baby Marrows (Courgettes)

Zucchini Ripieni

4 baby marrows or large courgettes	*4 tomatoes, chopped*
1 onion, chopped	*Breadcrumbs*
100g (4oz) minced beef or lamb	*Grated fresh Parmesan cheese*
1 tablespoon fresh parsley, chopped	*Salt and pepper*
	125ml (4fl oz) olive oil

Wash the marrows or courgettes and cook for 10 minutes in boiling, salted water. Drain, slice in half lengthways and scoop out the centres.

Heat the oil, lightly fry the onion and meat, add the parsley, tomatoes and scooped-out vegetable pulp. Season with salt and pepper and simmer for 15 minutes. Fill the marrow or courgette halves with this mixture, sprinkle with breadcrumbs and cheese and bake at 190°C/375°F/Gas 5 for 15 minutes.

Creamed Onions

Cipolle alla Crema

900g (2lb) small white onions	*Nutmeg*
150ml (1/4 pint) dry white wine	*1 tablespoon plain flour*
Salt and pepper	

Peel the onions and place them, whole, in a saucepan. Add salt and pepper and cover with cold water. Cook uncovered for 20 minutes. Add a flour and water paste to thicken the onion stock. Stir well until the sauce is thick, add the wine and a good pinch of nutmeg and continue to cook for another 10 minutes. Excellent with mutton.

Italian cooking

Stuffed Onions

Cipolle Ripiene

6 large onions
225g (8oz) potato purée
1 tablespoon tomato purée
4 tablespoons grated fresh
   Parmesan cheese

1 beaten egg
Salt and pepper
Soft breadcrumbs
Butter

Peel the onions and cook in plenty of boiling water for 15 minutes. Drain and place in cold water. Scoop out the centres, leaving a shell of 2 to 3 layers of onion. Chop the scooped-out onion and combine with the remaining ingredients except the breadcrumbs and butter. Refill the onions with this mixture, sprinkle with breadcrumbs, dot with butter and bake at 190°C/375°F/Gas 5 for 25 minutes.

Onions Cooked in Wine

Cipolle al Vino Bianco

450g (1lb) onions
300ml (1/2 pint) dry white wine
1 clove garlic, sliced

125ml (4fl oz) olive oil
Fresh thyme
Salt and pepper

Peel and slice the onions. Heat the oil and fry the onions with the garlic until they begin to brown. Add salt and pepper, thyme and wine. Simmer gently until the onions are soft.

Sour-Sweet Onions

Cipolle in Salsa Agrodolce

Peel 450g (1lb) of small onions and lightly brown them in a mixture of hot oil and butter. Add 150ml (1/4 pint) of dry white wine or tarragon vinegar, 2 heaped tablespoons of sugar and cook until the onions are soft.

Onion Flan

'Flan' di Cipolle

4 large onions	*125ml (4fl oz) olive oil*
Bacon rinds	*Salt and pepper*
175ml (6fl oz) single cream	*Plain flour*
2 eggs	*225g (8oz) short pastry (page 200)*

Line a flan tin with the pastry, leaving a good rim to make a neat edge. Bake 'blind' for a few moments.

Peel and slice the onions in rounds. Heat the oil, fry the bacon rinds and remove these when crisp. Fry the onions until a golden brown, sprinkle them with flour, and stir continuously. Add salt and pepper and gradually the cream. Continue to cook gently until the onions are creamy.

Remove the pan from the heat and cool the mixture a little. Beat the egg yolks and whites separately. Whip the yolks into the creamed onions, then fold in the whites. Pour this mixture into the flan case and bake at 190°C/375°F/Gas 5 for 20 minutes. Serve as an accompaniment to roast meat, or as a main course with a green salad.

Italian cooking

Fried Peppers

Peperoni Fritti

Wash as many peppers as required, remove the stalks and cut them into rounds. Cut out the core and wipe off all the seeds. Dip in beaten egg and fry in deep boiling oil until browned.

These are excellent served with a sour-sweet sauce.

Baked Potato Puff

Focaccia di Patate

900g (2lb) potatoes
50g (2oz) butter
300ml (1/2 pint) boiling milk
2 beaten egg whites
2 beaten egg yolks

125ml (4fl oz) gin
50g (2oz) sugar
Grated rind 1 lemon
Salt

Peel the potatoes, cut them into pieces of fairly equal size and cook in boiling salted water until very soft. Drain off the water and mash the potatoes until fluffy. Beat in the butter and milk, then the sugar, gin, salt, lemon rind and beaten yolks. Fold in the whites, very stiffly beaten, then pour the mixture into a greased soufflé dish. Bake at 190°C/375°F/Gas 5 for 10 minutes and serve at once.

Stuffed Baked Potatoes

Patate Farcite

Scrub as many large potatoes as required. Bake them at 230°C/450°F/Gas 8 until tender. While the potatoes are cooking prepare a stuffing. Combine some finely minced beef or lamb, chopped fresh parsley, soft breadcrumbs, grated fresh Parmesan cheese, salt, pepper and enough beaten egg to bind the mixture.

Cut the potatoes lengthways if they are very large or, if only of medium size, slice off the top, and scoop out the insides. Mash this with hot milk and butter and beat to a cream. Combine with the meat mixture and pile lightly into the potato shells. Place in a baking tin and cover each potato half with a thin slice of fresh Parmesan cheese. Bake at 190°C/375°F/Gas 5 for about 15 minutes or until the cheese has formed a light brown crust.

Scalloped Potatoes

Patate al Forno

450g (1lb) potatoes	1 tablespoon chopped fresh parsley
225g (8oz) courgettes	Grated fresh Parmesan cheese
1 large onion, chopped	Salt and pepper
3 large tomatoes	Brown breadcrumbs
1 clove garlic, chopped	Olive oil

Clean and peel all the vegetables and cut them into slices. Rub a pie dish, or a casserole, with oil leaving a filmy layer at the bottom. Arrange all the vegetables in alternate layers, add the garlic, very finely chopped, salt and pepper. Sprinkle each layer with cheese, parsley and breadcrumbs. Pour a little oil or melted butter over the top layer. Sprinkle lightly with cheese and breadcrumbs to form a thin crust and bake at 190°C/375°F/Gas 5 until all the vegetables are quite soft.

Italian cooking

Pumpkin, Sicilian Style

Zucca gialla alla Siciliana

900g (2lb) pumpkin
300ml (1/2 pint) dry white wine
2 sprigs fresh mint
1 teaspoon sugar
1 clove garlic (optional)

2 teaspoons olive oil
2 tablespoons lemon juice
125ml (4fl oz) single cream
Salt

Peel the pumpkin, cut it into strips, sprinkle with salt and leave for 1 hour.

Heat the oil in a saucepan, add the garlic, then the pumpkin. Brown a little, add the wine, sugar and mint and simmer gently until the pumpkin is tender but not squashy. Just before it is ready remove the mint, add the cream and lemon juice and continue to cook for another 5 minutes, stirring carefully all the time.

Purée of Dried Pulses
(Peas, Beans etc.)

Crema di Pisella, Fagioli Lenticchie

450g (1lb) green lentils	*1 hard-cooked egg yolk*
1 onion, chopped	*Salt and pepper*
1 stick celery, chopped	*2 cloves*
1 carrot, chopped	*1 clove garlic*
1 tomato, chopped	*Pinch bicarbonate of soda*
Bacon rinds	*English mustard powder*

Wash the lentils, cover with water and leave to soak overnight. Drain, cover again with cold water and bacon rinds, vegetables, cloves, bicarbonate of soda and garlic. Boil slowly until soft. Strain and rub everything through a sieve to a purée. Mash the egg yolk with salt, pepper and mustard and beat this into the purée. Continue beating until it is smooth and creamy.

Serve topped with slices of crisply fried onions and triangles of fried bread.

Chick-peas are particularly good cooked in this way.

Spinach with Cheese

Spinaci alla Parmigiana

Fry in butter for 15 minutes some cooked and chopped spinach, season with salt and pepper and flavour with nutmeg and grated fresh Parmesan cheese.

Italian cooking

Spinach with Anchovies

Spinaci all'Acciughe

900g (2lb) spinach
25g (1oz) butter
Pepper

5 anchovies
1 clove garlic, chopped

Wash the spinach and cook it without water or salt until soft. Drain and chop finely.

Melt the butter, add the anchovies and garlic and sauté for a few moments. Return the spinach to the pan, add pepper, stir and cook until the spinach is quite reheated. Serve with triangles of fried bread.

Salt is not necessary as the anchovies provide enough.

Spinach Flan

'Flan' di Spinaci

900g (2lb) spinach
50g (2oz) butter
300ml (1/2 pint) single cream
50g (2oz) plain flour
2 well-beaten eggs
1 large onion, finely chopped

Salt and pepper
Grated nutmeg
50g (2oz) grated fresh
   Parmesan cheese
225g (8oz) short pastry (page 200)

Make a flan case of short pastry and bake it 'blind'. Wash and pick over the spinach and partly cook it without water. Drain and chop finely.

Melt the butter and fry the onion to a golden brown. Sprinkle with flour, stir and cook for 3 minutes before pouring in the cream. Season well with salt and pepper and continue cooking very gently until the mixture is smooth and thick. Add the spinach and continue cooking until it is quite soft.

Remove from the heat, leave to cool, then beat in the cheese and eggs. Pour this mixture into the flan case, flavour slightly with nutmeg and bake at 230°C/450°F/Gas 8 for 15 to 20 minutes. Serve very hot.

Spinach Roman Style

Spinaci alla Romana

Fry some cooked and chopped spinach in olive oil with raisins, pine nuts, salt, pepper, spices and a very little chopped onion for 15 minutes.

Tomatoes Stuffed with Rice

Pomidoro Ripieni di Riso

8 tomatoes
175g (6oz) long-grain rice
Fresh parsley, chopped
1 clove garlic, chopped
A little butter or oil
1 onion, chopped

1 stick celery, chopped
1 carrot, chopped
Salt and pepper
Fresh mint
1 teaspoon sugar
Grated fresh Parmesan cheese

Wash the tomatoes, cut off the tops and scoop out the centres. Sprinkle the cases with salt, pepper and chopped fresh mint.

Heat the butter, or oil, and fry the onion, celery, carrot, parsley, garlic and scooped-out tomato. Simmer until soft, then pass this mixture through a sieve and combine with the rice. Half fill each tomato case with the rice, top with grated cheese and place in a baking tin. Pour into the tin enough boiling water to reach halfway up the sides of the tomatoes. Bake very slowly at 190°C/375°F/Gas 5 until the rice has cooked. If allowed to cook too quickly the rice will be hard and the tomatoes squashy.

If time is limited use cooked rice but in this case fill the tomato cases to the top.

Italian cooking

Tomato Flan

Focaccia di Pomidoro

900g (2lb) tomatoes
2 large onions, chopped
1 large courgette, sliced
Bacon rinds
Chopped fresh parsley
1–2 beaten eggs
Grated fresh Parmesan cheese

Pepper and salt
Fresh sage
1 teaspoon sugar
1 clove garlic, chopped
3 tablespoons olive oil
350g (12oz) short pastry
  (page 200)

Make enough short pastry to line a 25cm (10in) flan case and bake it 'blind' for 5 minutes.

Heat the oil and fry the bacon rinds with the onions and garlic. Remove the rinds when they are crisp. Add the tomatoes, peeled and sliced, plenty of parsley, the courgette, salt, pepper, sugar and a little sage. Simmer until everything is soft.

Pour this mixture into the flan case. Cover the top with the egg and sprinkle it with grated cheese. Bake at 220°C/425°F/Gas 7 until the pastry is a golden brown.

Buttered Turnips

Rape al Burro

Peel as many turnips as required and cut into thin rounds. Cook them gently in lightly salted, boiling water for 20 minutes. Drain and fry in butter on both sides.

When they are a golden brown, just before serving, sprinkle generously with grated fresh Parmesan cheese.

Egg and Cheese Dishes
Le Uova e Piatti di Formaggio

Italian cooking

Egg and Cheese Cream

Fonduta

4 egg yolks
350g (12oz) Fontina cheese,
   cut into cubes
Milk

25g (1oz) butter
Fried bread
White pepper
1 white truffle (optional)

This is Piedmont's most celebrated dish and must be made with Fontina cheese, one of Italy's great cheeses. In appearance it resembles Gruyère, with a firm texture and small holes. Fonduta must have Fontina to be genuine.

Soak the cheese in milk for several hours. Put the butter and the egg yolks into the top of a double pan and when the butter begins to change colour add the cheese. Stir until the cheese is completely melted, using a wooden spatula and never allowing the mixture to boil. When it is thick and creamy remove from the heat and add pepper. No salt is needed as the cheese contains enough. In Piedmont, white truffles, which are plentiful, are added towards the end of cooking time.

Serve in individual bowls with fingers of fried bread.

Eggs Fried with Cheese

Uova alla Parmigiana

Grease as many individual frying pans as required and drop 1 raw egg in each. Add plenty of salt, pepper and diced bacon, and completely smother each egg with grated fresh Parmesan cheese. Cook gently until the eggs are set, but not hard. Serve with fingers of fried bread.

Italian cooking

Poached Eggs with Salad Cream

Uova Apfogate Sui Crostini

4 eggs
25g (1oz) butter
150ml (1/4 pint) dry white wine

4 slices toast
Salad dressing

Melt the butter in a small saucepan, add the wine and blend together well. Break each egg separately in a cup and slip them, one at a time, into the wine. Poach each singly until the whites are firm. Carefully place each egg on a slice of toast and pour over each some fairly thin salad dressing. Serve hot.

Eggs Cooked in Sweet-Sour Sauce

Uova in Salsa Agrodolce

6 eggs
1 onion, chopped
2 bay leaves
2 cloves
150ml (1/4 pint) dry white wine
300ml (1/2 pint) vegetable stock

1 tablespoon sugar
Salt and pepper
50g (2oz) butter
Plain flour
1 tablespoon vinegar

Cook the eggs for 6 minutes exactly in boiling water, then plunge into cold water and you will find them fairly easy to peel, even though they are not hard-boiled.

Melt the butter and simmer the onion until soft. Sprinkle with flour, add salt and pepper, stir until smooth then gradually pour in the stock. Add cloves and bay leaves and simmer for 15 minutes. Strain through a fine sieve. Reheat, add the sugar and white wine, then the eggs. Simmer until the eggs are hard. Serve the eggs in the sauce with fried bread.

Eggs are equally good cooked this way in a tomato sauce.

Eggs with Peas and Tomatoes

Uova coi Piselli e Pomidori

Rather similar to the previous recipe. Fry in oil or butter a large chopped onion, a clove of garlic and 450g (1lb) of sliced tomatoes until very soft. Add 450g (1lb) of cooked green peas, salt and pepper. Drop in 6 shelled eggs, sprinkle with paprika and continue to cook until the eggs are set. An alternative way is to put the cooked peas and tomatoes into a casserole, make hollows into which to drop the eggs, sprinkle them with paprika and bake them at 190°C/375°F/Gas 5 until they are set.

Italian cooking

Eggs, Hunter's Style

Uova alla Cacciatora

6 eggs
6 chicken livers
1 tablespoon chopped green
  olives
1 small onion, grated
150ml (1/4 pint) dry white wine
300ml (1/2 pint) tomato juice

Fresh rosemary, basil and thyme
Salt and pepper
Butter
Plain flour
6 slices toast spread with
  liver pâté

Cut the livers into very small pieces and sauté them in butter. Add the onion, brown it and very lightly dust with flour. Stir and simmer for 5 minutes. Pour in the tomato juice, stir this well into the livers and onion, then add wine, herbs, olives and seasonings. Mix all these ingredients well, then add the eggs one by one. Continue to cook slowly until the eggs are set. Place eggs and livers on toast and cover with sauce.

Eggs Baked in Rice

Uova sul Riso

6 eggs
225g (8oz) long-grain rice
225g 8oz) tomatoes, chopped
Salt and pepper

1 small onion, chopped
75g (3oz) fresh Parmesan
  cheese, grated
Butter for frying

Throw the rice into salted, boiling water, and cook until tender. Drain. Fry the onion in butter until brown, add the tomatoes and cook them until soft. Stir to a pulp, add salt and pepper and rub through a sieve. Mix the rice, cheese and sauce together and turn this mixture into a greased and fairly shallow casserole. Make 6 hollows in the rice, drop an egg into each, sprinkle with salt, pepper and extra Parmesan cheese. Bake at 190°C/375°F/Gas 5 until the eggs are firm.

Eggs with Spinach

Uova Fiorentina

900g (2lb) cooked spinach
6 eggs
175g (6oz) fresh Parmesan
  cheese, grated

6 anchovies, chopped
Salt, black pepper and paprika

Chop the spinach finely, and put it into a shallow, greased casserole, preferably oblong in shape. Make 6 small wells in the spinach and drop an egg into each. Add seasonings. Garnish with anchovies and sprinkle with cheese. Bake at 190°C/375°F/Gas 5 until the eggs are set.

You can use individual ramekin dishes instead of a casserole, if you prefer it.

Eggs Poached in Tomato Sauce

Uova alla Pomidoro

4 eggs
450g (1lb) tomatoes
4 slices toast

2 tablespoons chopped fresh parsley
Salt and pepper
Butter

Peel and slice the tomatoes and simmer in butter with the parsley until soft. Add salt and pepper and stir. Make 4 wells in the tomato pulp and drop an egg into each. Continue cooking until the eggs are set. Serve each egg on a slice of toast and cover with sauce.

Italian cooking

Eggs in Tomato Cups

Uova alla Casalinga

6 eggs
6 large tomatoes

Salt and black pepper
Butter

Scoop out the centres of the tomatoes and bake them at 190°C/375°F/Gas 5 until they are almost soft, then drop an egg into each tomato. Sprinkle with salt and pepper, dot with butter and continue to bake until the eggs are set.

Omelette

Frittata

In Italy there are two distinct types of omelette as well as the many different flavourings for them. The first, the omelette proper, is made and folded like the French omelette. The second, and more usual version, is called a *frittata* and is not folded when cooked.

6 eggs
2 tablespoons milk

50g (2oz) butter for frying
Salt and pepper

Beat the eggs very slightly and combine with the milk and seasonings. Heat the butter in an omelette pan, pour just a little of it into the eggs, then pour the egg mixture into the pan. As the omelette begins to cook underneath, prick it with a fork and run a knife around the edges. When the underneath is a golden brown, fold the omelette over, and leave to set for 1 minute, then serve at once.

For flavouring combine the beaten eggs with any of the usual omelette flavourings, including chopped fresh mint, fresh tarragon, chopped fresh chervil, fresh parsley, shallots, chives, onion and carrot. Cottage cheese is a very usual Italian omelette ingredient, also dried mushrooms, dandelion tips, asparagus and, of course, cheese of all types.

The *frittata* is made with eggs beaten very lightly, just enough to mix the whites and the yolks. A little milk is added, also salt and pepper and melted butter. When it has been fried to a golden brown on one side, it is turned over, as with a pancake, and fried on the other side. Its texture is not unlike that of a scrambled egg.

I find it easier to brown the top of a *frittata* under a grill as turning requires considerable knack and skill.

With a *frittata* rather more unusual fillings are used. Here are just a few.

Omelette with Cheese and Tomatoes

Frittata alla Capagnola

Beat 4 eggs very lightly. Mix with grated fresh Parmesan cheese, salt and pepper. Heat 50g (2oz) of butter in an omelette pan and fry until soft 6 peeled and chopped tomatoes. Flavour them with chopped fresh mint, then pour over them the beaten eggs. Continue as instructed for *frittata*.

Macaroni Omelette

Frittata col Maccheroni alla Napoletana

100g (4oz) cooked macaroni	*1 teaspoon capers*
4 eggs	*Salt and pepper*
2 tablespoons single cream	*Grated fresh Parmesan cheese*
Handful chopped fresh parsley	*Butter for frying*

Lightly beat the eggs, adding cream, salt and pepper.

Melt some butter in a large omelette pan and very lightly fry the macaroni. Add parsley, cheese, and capers and then stir in the eggs. Cook on top of the stove until the egg mixture is firm, then put under the grill to get a good, almost crusty, top.

Italian cooking

Omelette, Savoy Style

Frittata alla Savoiarda

Beat lightly 4 eggs with salt and pepper and add a little milk. Fry lightly in butter 3 tablespoons of cold cooked potato, cut into cubes, and the same amount of bacon and Gruyère cheese. Continue as above.

Baked Cheese Omelette

Frittata con Formaggio al Forno

Break 4 egg yolks in a basin and combine them with 3 tablespoons of milk. Beat very lightly. Whisk the whites until stiff and fold them into the egg yolks. Add 2 tablespoons of grated Gruyère cheese and pour the mixture into a well-greased, shallow oven casserole. Bake at 190°C/375°F/Gas 5 until a golden brown.

Breadcrumb Omelette

Frittata alla Crostina

Beat lightly 4 eggs, adding salt and pepper but no milk. Sauté 3 tablespoons of white breadcrumbs in butter, cover with 2 tablespoons of single cream, then add the beaten eggs. Continue as for *frittata*.

Fried Bread, Neapolitan Style

Crostini alla Napoletana

Fry in butter as many slices of bread as required and brown both sides. Remove from the pan and keep hot. In the same butter fry an equal number of cheese slices, brown them on both sides and put a slice of cheese on each slice of bread. Fry several peeled and chopped tomatoes, with some finely chopped green peppers, flavour them with fresh marjoram, salt and pepper and simmer until the tomatoes are very soft. Cover the cheese and bread with tomato sauce and serve very hot.

Mozzarella Cheese Sandwiches

Mozzarella in Carrozza

Cut as many thin slices of bread as required, trim off the crusts and spread with melted butter. Make sandwiches using mozzarella cheese as a filling. Press the edges together very firmly. Beat 1 to 2 eggs, adding salt and pepper, and dip the sandwiches in the beaten egg. Fry on both sides until brown in either very hot butter or olive oil.

Instead of a coating of beaten egg, a coating of batter may be used.

Italian cooking

Tomato Pie (Pizza)

Pizza alla Napoletana

450g (1lb) plain flour
25g (1oz) dried yeast
900g (2lb) tomatoes
6 anchovies
1 clove garlic, chopped

100g (4oz) mozzarella cheese
Fresh marjoram, finely chopped
Olive oil
Salt and pepper

Dissolve the yeast in tepid water. Mix the flour with 1 tablespoon of olive oil, then add the dissolved yeast. Knead until the dough is smooth. Leave it in a covered bowl for 2 hours or until it has doubled its size.

Peel and chop the tomatoes. Heat 2 tablespoons of oil in a pan, add the tomatoes, garlic, salt and pepper. Cook gently for 30 minutes.

When the dough has risen, roll it until it is very thin and spread it over a large, well-oiled baking tin. The edges should be slightly thicker than the middle. Make slight indentations in the pastry. Spread it with the tomatoes. Slice the mozzarella and spread this over the top and garnish with anchovies. Bake at 230°C/450°F/Gas 8 for 10 minutes, reduce the heat to 190°C/375°F/Gas 5 and bake for a further 5 to 10 minutes.

This is one of the most usual of the many *pizza* which is today as popular outside of Italy as within the country. The word simply means pie, therefore it is not surprising that the recipes vary enormously, so do pies. There are *pizze* with onions and bacon, with cheese and tomatoes, with garlic and herbs. There are those with fish filling, and some which are sweet. Some are covered but most *pizze* are open, like a tart. There are also *pizze* which are made at home with puff or flaky pastry; these are usually called *alla casalinga*, or home-made.

Cheese Tart

Pizza alla Campofranco

Roll out fairly thinly 225g (8oz) of brioche pastry (page 186), and spread it over a greased baking sheet. Cover with thin slices of mozzarella cheese, sliced bacon and tomatoes. Sprinkle with grated fresh Parmesan cheese. Beat 1 to 2 eggs with salt and pepper until frothy and pour the mixture over the cheese. Bake at 190°C/375°F/Gas 5 until brown.

Pie with Yeast Pastry

Pizzadalina

Fresh yeast	*Anchovies*
900g (2lb) onions	*150g (5oz) black olives*
Butter	*3 cloves garlic*
Fresh Parmesan cheese	*Salt and pepper*
Fresh bay leaves, thyme, parsley	

Enough yeast dough is needed so that when pulled out it will cover a fairly large, round baking tin.

Peel and slice the onions and cook them in butter until they are very soft. Try to keep them white. Add the garlic and the herbs and remove these when the onions are cooked. Season with salt and pepper. Prick the dough all over with a fork, then cover it with the cooked onions. Add the olives, stoned and halved, then decorate the pie with fillets of anchovy. Bake the pie at 230°C/450°F/Gas 8 until a golden brown. It should take about 30 minutes.

Puff pastry can be used instead of fresh yeast.

Italian cooking

Easter Cake

Torta Pasqualina

Plain flour
450g (1lb) beetroot leaves
6 eggs
Handful chopped fresh parsley
1 chopped onion
75g (3oz) grated fresh Parmesan
   cheese

225g (8oz) curd cheese
200ml (7fl oz) single cream
Olive oil
50g (2oz) butter
Salt and pepper
Fresh marjoram

Mix 450g (1lb) of sieved flour with 1 tablespoon of olive oil and enough warm water to make a smooth and pliable dough. Divide this into 30 pieces, shape them into balls, and leave them for 1 hour in a cool place, well-covered with a damp cloth.

Cut away the spine from each of the beetroot leaves, then roll each one separately as when rolling cigarettes, then with sharp kitchen scissors cut each roll into pieces, roughly 6mm (1/4in) wide. Unroll each piece, they will look like noodles, wash them well and leave them to dry.

Melt the butter, very lightly fry the leaves, add the parsley, salt, pepper, onion, Parmesan cheese and marjoram. Leave this on the side of the stove until needed.

Beat into the curd cheese 3 tablespoons of sieved flour, and when this mixture is smooth dilute it with the cream, and a few drops of olive oil. Put aside until needed, covered with a cloth.

Roll out separately 15 of the balls of dough. Each should be the same size and rolled as thinly as possible. Grease a flat baking tin, and line the bottom with one of the pieces of dough. Brush this lightly with olive oil and cover it with another piece of dough. Continue to do this until all the 15 pieces are neatly piled up one on top of the other.

Spread the top layer with the beetroot mixture, cover this with the curd cheese. With the back of a spoon make 'wells' in the cheese and into each 'well' drop 1 raw egg. In between the eggs place thin slivers of butter.

Roll out the remaining pieces of dough, and pile these on top of the rest, brushing each layer with olive oil. Trim round the sides and with the pieces make an edge for the top layer. Prick the top with a fork to prevent blistering and bake at 190°C/375°F/Gas 5 for 1 hour.

Salads
Insalata

Italian cooking

Cabbage Salad

Insalata di Cavoli

Wash well 1 small white cabbage and cook in slightly salted water. Drain it and shred it finely.

Rub a wooden salad bowl with garlic and add the shredded cabbage.

Make a dressing with 3 parts Italian olive oil to 1 part tarragon vinegar and salt and black pepper to taste. Gradually add 2 well-beaten eggs and 225ml (8fl oz) of single cream. Cook the dressing very slowly over boiling water until it thickens.

Pour the dressing while still hot over the cabbage and leave to cool. Garnish with anchovies and crisply fried parsley.

For successful frying, parsley must be very fresh and crisp. Drop into deep boiling fat for just 1 minute. If you tie a piece of cotton to the stems it makes it easier to pull the parsley quickly out of the fat, when it is done.

Celery Salad

Insalata di Sedano

Thoroughly wash and chop a head of celery, or, better still, just the heart, and the same amount of chicory. Mix with a dressing of oil and vinegar and sprinkle with 2 tablespoons of Italian prosciutto or its equivalent. Chill, and just before serving add a tablespoon of salad cream. Add salt and pepper to taste.

Italian cooking

Chicory Salad

Insalata di Cicoria

Wash 2 crisp heads of chicory, remove any bruised or broken leaves, then chop the rest into small rounds. Mix with a little sliced garlic, some chopped green olives and Italian Dressing (page 210).

In Italy, and especially in Piedmont, chopped white truffles are added. But in Britain or elsewhere a few green peas can add flavour and colour to the salad, or a teaspoon of chopped, hot red peppers can be used.

Christmas Eve Salad

Insalata di Rinforz

Very thoroughly wash a large, white cauliflower and soak it head down for 30 minutes in cold, salted water. Divide it into flowerets and cook for 10 to 15 minutes in boiling salted water. Put the flowerets into a salad bowl previously rubbed with garlic, then pour over them enough Italian Dressing (page 210) to coat each piece. Toss briskly, but not so violently that the cauliflower becomes mashed, then add 6 stoned black olives and 1 heaped tablespoon of capers.

Chill before serving.

It is usual to serve this salad with carp or eel, and in Naples it is served on Christmas Eve.

Fennel Salad

Insalata Finnocchi

Select 2 very white and crisp bulbs of fennel. Trim and slice them into lengths, they should be rather thin. Toss lightly in salad oil and serve cold.

Gipsy Salad

Insalata Gipsy

1 red, 1 green and 1 yellow
  pepper
1 peeled tomato
1 onion
1 stick celery
1 head chicory
4 radishes

4 anchovies
2 tablespoons capers
1 sprig fresh basil
1 sprig fresh mint
1 clove garlic, chopped
Pepper and English mustard powder
125ml (4fl oz) olive oil

Chop the vegetables and anchovies and toss them very lightly with a wooden spoon. Add herbs, garlic, capers and seasonings, then gradually the olive oil. Chill and serve with boiled meats.

Lettuce Salad

Insalata di Lattughe

To make a good lettuce salad all the ingredients must first be chilled. Only wash the lettuce if it is absolutely necessary and, if you do, make sure it is perfectly dry. This can be done either in a salad spinner or by drying with a linen cloth. Pull the lettuce apart with your hands, do not use a knife.

Have ready a wooden salad bowl and rub it lightly first with salt, then with cut garlic, as much as desired. Put the lettuce in the bowl and sprinkle it with finely grated onion and black pepper. Pour over it a plain olive oil and tarragon vinegar dressing and toss briskly until each leaf is coated with the dressing.

If you want a crisp salad serve at once. But if you prefer, as many Continental people do, a rather wilted affair, then leave it for a short while before serving.

Italian cooking

Haricot Bean Salad

Insalata di Fagiolini

Soak 225g (8oz) haricot beans overnight. Next day cook them until soft in fresh, salted water to which a teaspoon of bicarbonate of soda has been added. Drain, and remove any beans that are too soft and dry.

Chop very finely 1 small onion, 1 clove of garlic, a little fresh sage, parsley, tarragon, sweet basil and rosemary and mix with 1 heaped tablespoon of tinned tuna fish. Toss all this together with a spoon then add 3 tablespoons of olive oil and 1 of vinegar mixed together.

Mix this dressing with the beans, sprinkle with pepper and serve garnished with strips of anchovy.

Vegetable Salad

Cappon Magro

Salad

1 small cauliflower
225g (8oz) green peas
225g (8oz) French beans
225g (8oz) potatoes
4 carrots
1 stick celery

A few radishes
100g (4oz) mushrooms
1 clove garlic
1 large dry bread cracker
Mixed fish (optional)

Dressing

2 tablespoons chopped fresh parsley
100g (4oz) grated fennel (optional)
4 tablespoons capers
8 anchovies, chopped

2 hard-boiled egg yolks
2 tablespoons soft breadcrumbs
Oil and lemon
Salt and pepper

Cook all the vegetables until tender. Divide the cauliflower into clusters, slice the carrots, potatoes, radishes and mushrooms. Break the beans into halves and chop the celery. Rub the dry bread cracker with garlic and, using this as a base, arrange all the vegetables on top, pyramid fashion, making an effective display of colour. In between, if available, put pieces of lobster, or shrimps, anchovies, smoked salmon or even smoked oysters.

Mash the garlic to a paste, add the remaining ingredients for the dressing and continue to mash until all are well-blended and the paste is smooth. Gradually add oil and lemon and work the paste to a cream. Pour this over the salad. Surround the base with more lobster, shrimps, etc.

Tuscan Salad (Bread Salad)

'Panzanella' alla Marinna

2 slices white bread
Chopped fresh basil
Handful chopped fresh parsley
1 tablespoon capers
Tarragon vinegar

4 Anchovies
2 chilli peppers
2 cloves garlic
Salt and black pepper
Oil

Soak the bread in water, squeeze it quite dry and crumble it finely. Mix with basil, parsley, capers, salt and pepper and just enough oil and vinegar mixed to moisten it. Put this aside while you prepare the dressing.

Crush the garlic to a paste, add the anchovies and peppers and work to a smooth paste. Add some vinegar to this until it is a creamy, but fairly thin, dressing.

Arrange the bread salad on a plate, surround it with slices of hard-boiled egg or sliced tomato, pour the dressing over the salad, chill and serve.

Give this salad a trial, even though it seems unusual at first sight. It is typical of Mediterranean salads, really very good, and rather a welcome change from the eternal lettuce, tomato and cucumber.

Italian cooking

Italian Potato Salad

Insalata di Patate

8 potatoes, cooked in their skins
1 large onion, chopped
2 hard-boiled eggs, chopped
1 green pepper, chopped
4 anchovies, chopped

Salt and pepper
2 lettuce hearts
1 clove garlic
Italian Dressing (page 210)

Peel the potatoes and cut them into cubes or slices. Mix with onion, eggs, pepper, anchovies and seasoning and add a little dressing. Wash and dry the lettuce hearts, separating the leaves. Rub a wooden bowl with garlic, arrange the lettuce at the bottom, add a little Italian dressing, toss until all the leaves are well-coated, then cover with the potato salad.

Chill before serving.

Sweet-Sour Potato Salad

Insalata di Patate Agrodolce

6 large potatoes cooked in their
  skins
1 onion, chopped
1 stick celery, chopped
2 hard-boiled eggs, chopped
1 gherkin, chopped
1 tablespoon fresh parsley,
  chopped

3 rashers diced bacon
100g (4oz) sugar
Salt and pepper
125ml (4fl oz) tarragon vinegar
2 beaten eggs
1/4 teaspoon English mustard
  powder
Olive oil for frying

Peel the potatoes and either slice them or cut into cubes. Mix with the onion, celery, hard-boiled eggs, gherkin and parsley.

Blend the vinegar with the beaten eggs and blend in 125ml (4fl oz) of water. Add the sugar, salt, pepper and mustard. Heat a little oil and fry the bacon until crisp, then add the egg and vinegar mixture. Simmer over boiling water until the mixture thickens, stirring all the while to prevent curdling. Pour it over the potato salad while still hot, toss lightly and serve.

Onion Salad

Insalata di Cipolle

Boil in salted water as many onions as required until they are almost tender. Drain, cut into slices and leave to dry. Pour over them enough Italian Dressing (page 210) to coat each onion slice. Serve garnished with fresh watercress and surrounded with slices of cold potatoes previously dipped in the dressing.

Italian cooking

Pastry, Cakes, Biscuits and Sweets
I Dolci

Sweet Almond Biscuits

Amaretti

225g (8oz) ground almonds
50g (2oz) plain flour
75g (3oz) caster sugar

1 beaten egg
1 teaspoon grated lemon rind
2 teaspoons lemon juice

Pound the almonds with the sugar until fine, then mix with the flour and the lemon rind. Beat the egg and lemon juice together and stir into the almond mixture. Knead to a paste. Add more egg if necessary as the paste should not be too firm. Form into small round balls and place on a greased baking sheet and bake at 180°C/350°F/Gas 4 until the biscuits are brown and crisp.

'Dead Men's Beans'

Fave dei Mort

These morbidly named cakes are popular throughout Italy, and are eaten traditionally on All Souls' Day, 2 November. Their origin is somewhat obscure, and recipes for them are to be found in all parts of Italy. In many countries, in more ancient times, beans were connected with death and with the souls of the departed. Despite their origin and name these 'beans' are extremely pleasant and the two recipes I have chosen from a dozen or more are probably two of the most simple.

Recipe 1

Cream 50g (2oz) of butter with 50g (2oz) of sugar. Add 1 egg and continue beating until the mixture is smooth. Gradually work in 225g (8oz) of plain flour and 1 teaspoon of baking powder. Add 125ml (4fl oz) of rum and enough cold water to make a stiff dough. Roll on to a floured board to a thickness of about 1cm (1/2in). Cut off small pieces and shape these into beans. Brush each lightly with beaten egg and bake at 190°C/375°F/Gas 5 until a golden brown.

Recipe 2

Pound 100g (4oz) of blanched and ground almonds with 100g (4oz) of sugar until fine. Add 175g (6oz) of sieved flour. Rub in well 25g (1oz) of butter, then add 1 beaten egg and enough brandy and water to make a firm dough. Shape as above into beans, brush with beaten egg and bake until a golden brown at 190°C/375°F/Gas 5.

Sweet Brioche

Panettone di Milano

This sweet brioche is a speciality of Milan, and owes its name to its history. The first Panettone was said to have been made by a baker called Toni. It became very popular but it had no special name, so purchasers simply asked for Panettone, Toni's bread. To enjoy it thoroughly one should, of course, sit outside a Milan café, eating Panettone hot and crisp and sipping with it a glass of white wine.

100g (4oz) plain flour	50g (2oz) candied peel
15g (1/2oz) dried yeast	Rind 1 lemon
50g (2oz) butter	50g (2oz) sugar
3 egg yolks	Salt
75g (3oz) raisins	150ml (1/4 pint) milk

Chop the peel very finely. Warm the milk, add the butter and the yeast, stir until smooth and then leave to rise for 20 minutes.

Sieve half the flour into a bowl, add the eggs, sugar and salt, mix well, then beat thoroughly. Add the remaining flour, the yeast mixture, the raisins, peel, lemon rind and mix everything together. Knead to a firm dough. This you must do for at least 5 minutes, then leave covered with a cloth for about 2 hours. Grease some bun tins, divide the dough into pieces, half fill each tin, and then leave until the dough has risen to twice its original size. Brush with beaten egg. Put the tins into a hot oven (230°C/450°F/Gas 8), and leave them for 10 minutes by which time they will have started to change colour. Lower the heat to just moderate (190°C/375°F/Gas 5) and leave for another 20 minutes.

This recipe for Panettone is one of the simplest. 'Toni' obviously allowed variations in his bread, for some of the recipes tell you to use as many as 8 eggs.

Italian Cheesecake

Torta di Ricotta

Make enough short pastry to line a 23cm (9in) flan tin. When mixing the pastry add sherry as well as water. It is not necessary to bake it blind first.

Short pastry (page 200)	*1 tablespoon currants*
450g (1lb) cottage cheese	*1 teaspoon vanilla essence*
1 tablespoon chopped	*3 eggs*
candied peel	*100g (4oz) sugar*

Beat the cheese vigorously with a wooden spoon until creamy. Whisk the eggs until they are frothy, add the sugar and the vanilla essence, then beat into the cheese. Continue beating until these ingredients are well-blended, adding as you beat, the currants and the peel.

Fill the flan case with the cheese mixture. Bake at 240°C/475°F/Gas 9 for 10 minutes, then reduce the heat to 190°C/375°F/Gas 5 and bake for another 30 minutes or until the cheese filling is set.

Turn off the heat, open the oven door and leave the flan there for about an hour. It should be quite cold before cutting.

Italian cooking

Sicilian Cheesecake

Cassata alla Siciliana

25cm (10in) round sponge cake,
  ready made
450g (1lb) cottage cheese
100g (4oz) sugar

100g (4oz) bitter chocolate,
  grated
2 tablespoons maraschino
50g (2oz) glazed fruit

Beat the cheese (using a wooden spoon), until it is light and feathery, then rub it through a fine sieve to make it even more so. Add the sugar, the chocolate, the maraschino and half of the fruit, previously chopped. Continue to beat until the mixture is creamy.

Cut the sponge cake into 3 layers. Spread the creamed cheese thickly between the layers, but not on the top. This should be sprinkled only with vanilla sugar and decorated with the remaining fruit. Chill before serving.

For the sponge cake, the recipe for *Pan di Spagna* (page 193) is suitable.

Cats' Tongues

Lingue di Gatto

75g (3oz) plain flour
25g (1oz) butter
75g (3oz) vanilla sugar

3 egg whites
Lemon juice

Beat the butter and the sugar to a white cream, add the egg whites, stiffly beaten, then gradually add the flour and a few drops of lemon juice.

Grease a baking sheet and force the mixture through a pastry tube on to the baking sheet, leaving plenty of room between each tongue to allow the mixture to spread. Bake at 150°C/300°F/Gas 2 until the edges begin to turn a golden brown

These are delicious with stewed fruit, ice-cream or mousse.

Chestnut Flour Cake

Castagnaccio

Mix together 150g (5oz) of chestnut flour, a pinch of salt and 2 tablespoons of almond oil. Blend well and stir in just enough boiling water to make a pouring consistency. Pour into a greased, square, flat tin and sprinkle generously with pine nuts, sultanas, raisins and rosemary. This last ingredient is most important as its flavour is characteristic of the *Castagnaccio*.

Bake at 190°C/375°F/Gas 5 for 45 minutes, by which time the cake should be rather crumbly.

Chestnut flour is usually available in continental food stores.

Italian cooking

Easter Cake

Presnitz

This quite delicious pastry originates from Castagnevizza, but has been adopted by the inhabitants of Trieste as their own.

225g (8oz) puff pastry, ready
  made
75g (3oz) sultanas
75g (3oz) mixed nuts
50g (2oz) candied peel
75g (3oz) raisins
50g (2oz) sugar

50g (2oz) stale sponge
  cake
225ml (8fl oz) rum
1 egg
15g (1/2oz) butter
Lemon
Cinnamon

Soak the raisins with the sultanas in rum until they are completely round and smooth. Crumble the sponge cake into fine crumbs, coarsely grind the nuts, chop the peel and mix all these ingredients together, finally adding the rum-soaked fruit and any remaining rum. Stir until all the rum is absorbed, and add a squeeze of lemon juice and the sugar.

    Roll out the pastry in a strip 7.5cm (3in) wide and 1cm (1/2in) thick. Cover it with the rum-soaked mixture. Beat the egg and the butter together until smooth and then brush this over the top. Sprinkle very lightly with ground cinnamon, place on a flat greased baking sheet, and bake at 250°C/450°F/Gas 8 until the pastry is a golden brown. Serve very fresh, either hot or cold. It is best eaten the day it is made.

Italian Rum Cake

Zuppa Inglese

Zuppa, literally, means soup, but this sweet is anything but souplike. It is based on the English trifle or tipsy cake but is, in my opinion, very much better.

450g (1lb) sponge cake   *300ml (1/2 pint) whipping cream*
Zabaglione cream (page 207)   *Glazed fruits*
225ml (8fl oz) rum

Cut the sponge cake into 3 layers. Put the bottom layer on the dish in which you are going to serve the sweet. Pour over it 90ml (3fl oz) of rum and then spread it thickly with zabaglione cream. Add the second layer and repeat the process. Cover with the third layer, and pour the remaining rum over it but no cream.

Put the cake into the refrigerator until ready to serve. Spread the cream over the top and sides and garnish with chopped glazed fruits before serving.

It should be firm and should cut like a layer cake.

Paradiso Cake

Torta Paradiso

A favourite cake with Italians and one that their cooks seem to make with ease. It is usually served simply sprinkled with vanilla sugar, but occasionally cut into layers and filled with cream.

5 eggs	1 tablespoon lemon juice
150g (5oz) sugar	75g (3oz) plain flour

Separate the whites from the yolks of the eggs. Beat the yolks vigorously with the lemon juice and sugar, using a fairly large bowl. Place the bowl over a saucepan of boiling water, and gently cook, stirring all the while until the mixture thickens. Leave to cool.

Beat the whites until they are stiff then fold them into the creamed yolks. Gradually add the flour, doing this carefully, and when the cake mixture is well-blended pour into a greased and floured sponge cake tin and bake at 190°C/375°F/Gas 5 until a light brown. Leave the cake in the tin until cool.

Margaret Cake

Torta Margherita

150g (5oz) potato flour	1 teaspoon vanilla sugar
150g (5oz) caster sugar	1 teaspoon lemon sugar
4 eggs	

Separate the eggs and beat the yolks with the sugar. If you have the strength beat for 30 minutes! Gradually add the flour and continue beating until the mixture is very smooth. Whisk the egg whites until stiff, but not dry, and then fold them into the cake mixture. Pour this into a greased and floured cake tin.

Bake the cake for 5 minutes at 240°C/475°F/Gas 9, half remove it from the oven and very quickly make a cross on the top of it. Return it to the oven and bake it in the same heat for another 5 minutes. Then reduce the heat to 190°C/375°F/Gas 5 and continue to bake for another 30 minutes or until the cake is cooked through.

Do not take the cake from the tin until it is quite cold. Serve it either sprinkled with vanilla or lemon sugar, or spread with fresh cream and nuts. This type of cake is garnished very much as the individual cook fancies, although the basic cake is always made in the same way.

Sponge Cake

Pan di Spagna

100g (4oz) plain flour
4 eggs
100g (4oz) caster sugar

1 teaspoon almond flavouring
1 teaspoon grated lemon rind

Sift the flour 3 times. Separate the eggs, and beat the yolks and 75g (3oz) of the sugar together until smooth. Add the lemon rind and the flavouring.

Beat the whites until fairly stiff, add the rest of the sugar, and continue beating to a meringue consistency.

Gradually add the flour to the egg yolks, beating vigorously all the time, then fold in the egg whites. Pour the mixture into a well-greased sponge cake tin and bake for about 45 minutes at 190°C/375°F/Gas 5. Leave to cool in the tin.

Chestnut Flan

'Flan' di Castagne

Line a flan tin with short pastry and bake blind for 10 minutes.

Roast 900g (2lb) of chestnuts for about 15 minutes, having made a slit in their shells. Remove the outer shell and inner skin, then put into a pan with 150ml (¼ pint) of milk, 100g (4oz) of sugar and a little vanilla essence. Cook gently until soft. Press through a ricer then beat 2 to 3 egg yolks vigorously into them. Pile this mixture into the flan case and cover with meringue, made from 3 egg whites and 75g (3oz) of sugar. Bake at 190°C/375°F/Gas 5 until the meringue is just lightly browned.

Italian cooking

Prune Flan

Budino di Prugne

This is a wonderful way of preparing prunes and one which makes a delicious sweet.

225g (8oz) short pastry (page 200)
275g (10oz) prunes, soaked
75g (3oz) mixed dried fruits
  (sultanas, currants, raisins, etc.)
75g (3oz) mixed ground nuts

50g (2oz) sugar
100g (4oz) stale cake crumbs
2 tablespoons single cream
1 tablespoon grated lemon rind
125ml (4fl oz) brandy

Line a flan tin with the pastry. Soak the prunes overnight, then cook them in a little water, adding, just before they are ready, the dried fruit. Drain, stone and chop finely. Mix with the remaining ingredients. Cool, then put into the flan case. Flute the edges, sprinkle some nuts or crumbs on the top and bake at 220°C/425°F/Gas 7 for about 30 minutes, or until the pastry is a golden brown. Serve either hot or cold.

Fried Lovers' Knots

Cenci

225g (8oz) plain flour
25g (1oz) butter
50g (2oz) caster sugar

1 whole egg plus 1 yolk
2 tablespoons brandy

Sieve the flour and rub in the butter. Add the remaining ingredients and work the mixture to a rather stiff but very pliable dough.

Leave for 30 minutes wrapped in a cloth in a cool place. Roll out very thinly, almost to paper thinness, then cut into long, ribbon-like strips. Carefully tie these into lovers' knots and quickly fry them in deep, boiling fat until they are a golden brown.

Spread the *Cenci* on absorbent paper to drain away excess fat, sprinkle with caster sugar and serve hot, either alone or with fruit salad, cold mousse or a similar type of sweet.

Batter Fritters

Le Castagnole

1 egg
Plain flour
Sugar

Grated Lemon rind
Salt
Olive oil

Many Italian provinces claim these delicious batter fritters as their own invention. Certainly they are easily obtained in Rome.

Exact amounts for the ingredients cannot be given, but, even so, the fritters are easy enough to prepare.

Beat the egg in a large bowl with 1 tablespoon of fine sugar, about 1 tablespoon of oil, and a pinch of salt and lemon rind to flavour. When these ingredients are thoroughly blended, add enough sieved flour to make a paste of 'dropping' consistency. Work this until it is almost velvety in texture.

Have ready a pan with plenty of boiling hot oil and drop the paste into this in spoons, not too many at a time as the fritters will swell. Fry them until they are a golden brown, then take them out with a perforated spoon and place them on absorbent paper to drain off the surplus fat. Sprinkle with caster sugar and lemon juice and serve as hot as possible. Sometimes *Le Castagnole* are served with a thin jam or chocolate sauce.

Chestnut Fritters

Fritelle di Castagne

Prepare a chestnut purée as for a chestnut flan (page 193), and leave it to become very cold. A few hours in the refrigerator is ideal. Break off pieces about the size of a walnut and shape into balls. Roll in beaten egg and breadcrumbs and fry in deep fat until brown. Drain off excess fat on absorbent paper, sprinkle the fritters with vanilla sugar and serve hot. Sometimes these fritters are served with a thin chocolate sauce.

Italian cooking

Apple Fritters

Fritelle di Mele

Make a coating batter (page 207).

Peel and core 3 to 4 large cooking apples, and cut them into thick slices. Rub each slice with lemon, sprinkle generously with caster sugar and leave to soak for about 30 minutes in rum or brandy. Dip each slice into the batter and fry in deep, boiling fat until a pale amber colour. Drain off excess fat on to absorbent cooking paper, sprinkle with vanilla sugar and serve at once.

Sweet Fried Pastry Balls

Zeppole alla Napoletana

100g (4oz) plain flour	Oil for frying
300ml (1/2 pint) water	Sugar icing
150ml (1/4 pint) brandy	Salt

Put the flour into a saucepan and gradually stir in the water; when well-blended, add the brandy and a pinch of salt. Cook over a slow heat, stirring all the time, until the mixture comes away from the sides of the saucepan. Remove from the heat, allow to cool and then knead the dough until it is elastic and pliable.

Roll it into a long baton and cut into slices. Form each slice into a ball and fry in deep boiling fat until brown. Turn the balls from time to time so that they are equally browned all over.

Take from the pan with a perforated spoon and place on absorbent paper to drain off the excess oil. Roll in sieved icing sugar and serve hot.

These are a St Joseph's Day speciality.

Horseshoe Crisps

Cornetti

Use about 225g (8oz) of ready made puff pastry. Roll it out very thinly and cut it into strips. Shape the strips into horseshoes with the ends turned inside the shoe. Brush lightly with melted butter and dredge with caster sugar. Bake on a greased baking sheet at 190°C/375°F/Gas 5 until crisp and fairly dark brown. Take them from the oven and, while still hot, sprinkle with a little vanilla sugar. Leave until cold before serving.

They are specially good with morning coffee.

Pastry Roll with Honey and Nuts

Pizza 'Figliata'

Make a rich, short pastry (page 200) using eggs and sherry in the mixing. Roll it thinly, then brush with honey. Sprinkle generously with chopped mixed nuts (walnuts, almonds, hazelnuts, etc.) and chopped candied peel. Dredge lightly with mixed cake spice and shape into a spiral.

Bake at 190°C/375°F/Gas 5 for about 20 minutes. This roll is useful for morning coffee or children's teas.

Italian cooking

St Joseph's Day Fritters

Fritelle di San Giuseppe

The Feast Day of St Joseph, patron saint of hearth and home, is celebrated with much eating and ceremony. In Sicily it is the tradition for the rich to give a party on this day and to invite all their less wealthy neighbours; by the same tradition the tables should literally groan with good food. As a result, quite a number of dishes are accepted as St Joseph's Day specialities. Cheese seems to be banned on this particular Saint's day, and is not served even with the rich soups and the many pasta dishes that are eaten. It is made up for by many sweets.

St Joseph's Day fritters are made with rice, and you should start preparing them the day before they are to be eaten.

Cook 100g (4oz) long-grain rice slowly in 600ml (1 pint) of milk until the rice is very soft and has absorbed all the milk. Sweeten with sugar. Flavour with vanilla sugar or vanilla essence and 1 tablespoon of grated lemon rind, or orange and lemon rind mixed. Cool, then beat in 2 whole eggs and 50g (2oz) of potato flour. If this type of flour is not available then ordinary white flour will do. Add 125ml (4fl oz) of Marsala. Leave to stand overnight or for several hours in a refrigerator then shape into croquettes. Fry in deep boiling fat until golden brown.

Serve sprinkled with sugar. The croquettes are rather better, and easier to fry, if rolled first in egg and breadcrumbs.

Poor Knights of Windsor

Panorato alla Romana

This recipe seems to turn up in every country, probably because it is easy to make, cheap to prepare and most people appear to like it.

Slices of bread	Vanilla, sugar or cinnamon
Egg	Lemon juice
Milk	Butter for frying
Sugar	

Exact amounts depend on personal needs.

Soak the bread in slightly sweetened milk for 15 minutes. Sprinkle with lemon juice, then lay the slices carefully in beaten egg. Leave them until they have completely absorbed the egg, turning them once during the process.

Have ready a pan with melted hot butter and carefully place the bread in the pan. Fry on both sides until brown. Sprinkle with vanilla sugar or cinnamon and serve hot. The fried slices can be served alone or with stewed fruit.

Stale slices of bread are the best, cut neither too thick nor too thin and with the crusts cut off before soaking. For 12 slices of bread one needs 2 eggs. The finished slices should be fairly crisp on the outside but soft inside.

Rice Pudding, Italian Style

Torta di Riso

100g (4oz) pudding rice	*75g (3oz) candied fruit*
1.2 litres (2 pints) milk	*Vanilla essence*
25g (1oz) butter	*Pinch salt*
25g (1oz) ground almonds	*Grated orange peel*
75g (3oz) sugar	

Boil the rice for about 3 minutes in 1.2 litres (2 pints) of water, drain and leave to cool. Bring the milk with the almonds and orange peel to the boil and throw in the rice, afterwards adding the butter and the salt. Let the milk boil quickly for 10 minutes, then add the sugar and vanilla essence. Pour into a well-buttered dish and bake at 180°C/350°F/Gas 4 for 1 hour.

Decorate with candied peel before serving, and with whipped cream if desired.

Italian cooking

Sugar Syrup

Sciroppo di Zuchero

Put 225g (8oz) of sugar into a saucepan with 300ml (1/2 pint) of cold water and bring very slowly to boiling point. Take off any scum from the top, then cover, and boil quickly for 5 minutes. Reduce the heat, and continue to cook, still boiling but more gently, for another 25 minutes. Remove from the stove and cool. The syrup may be stored for future use in glass jars.

Short Pastry *(Italian)*

Pasta Frolla

225g (8oz) sieved plain flour	2 egg yolks
100g (4oz) butter	Cinnamon or grated lemon rind
75g (3oz) sugar	Salt

With the tips of the fingers or with a knife lightly work the butter into the flour until it has all but disappeared. Add the sugar, salt and cinnamon or lemon rind. Of the latter you need only enough to give the faintest flavour. When all these ingredients are well-blended, make a well in the centre, drop in the eggs, and mix to a paste with a wooden spoon. Add enough ice-cold water to make a firm dough, and then, if you have time, wrap the pastry in a cloth and leave it in a refrigerator until the next day, this will greatly improve the pastry.

This pastry is suitable for sweet tarts, pies, flans, etc. When making tarts the Italians use their imagination, putting in plenty of fruit and cream, nuts and flavouring.

St Joseph's Puffs

Sfenci di San Giuseppe

175g (6oz) plain flour	1 teaspoon grated lemon rind
75g (3oz) butter	1 teaspoon grated orange rind
3 eggs	Salt
300ml (1/2 pint) water	Cheese filling
1 teaspoon baking powder	

Sift the flour twice. Put the water, butter and a pinch of salt into a saucepan and bring slowly to the boil stirring all the time. Add all the flour at once, still stirring, then remove the mixture from the heat and beat vigorously. Lower the heat and continue to cook slowly, stirring all the time, until the mixture comes away from the sides of the pan. Leave to cool until it is just warm.

Separate the eggs and add the yolks one by one to the paste beating each in thoroughly. Add the baking powder, grated orange and lemon rind, and finally the egg whites, beaten very stiff. Drop the mixture in tablespoons on to a greased baking sheet and bake first for 10 minutes at 240°C/475°F/Gas 9, then for about 30 minutes at 190°C/375°F/Gas 5 until the puffs are a delicate golden brown.

Immediately upon taking them from the oven open them up through the centre to allow the steam to escape. Cool and fill with a cheese filling exactly similar to that used in *Cassata alla Siciliana* (page 188).

Baked Apples

Mele al Forno

Scoop out the centres of as many large and firm apples as required. Sprinkle the insides with sugar, and push into each a stick of bitter chocolate leaving about 1cm (1/2in) of it showing above the apples. Pour over them some Marsala, and bake at 190°C/375°F/Gas 5 until the apples are cooked through, basting from time to time with Marsala.

Italian cooking

Stuffed Dates

Datteri Farciti

Dates fresh from the trees are, of course, ideal for this recipe, but as these are usually difficult to obtain, good quality boxed dates can be used. Stone them with care and stuff them with the following mixture.

Crush 75–100g (3–4oz) of pistachio nuts with 50g (2oz) of sugar. Moisten with sherry, brandy or rum, and work to a soft paste, like almond paste. Fill each date with some of this filling. It should be enough for about 24 large dates. Garnish each date with half a blanched walnut.

Brandied Chestnuts

Castagne alla Fiamma

Bake 450g (1lb) of large chestnuts until they can be peeled with ease. Make about 225ml (8fl oz) of sugar syrup (page 200) and simmer the chestnuts in this until the syrup is completely absorbed.

Arrange the chestnuts in a silver serving dish, pour some warmed and really good brandy over them and set them alight just before serving.

Chestnut Purée with Coffee Cream

Dolci di Castagne

Make some chestnut purée (page 193), but mix some well-flavoured liqueur with it. Cherry brandy or maraschino is the Italian choice. Pile the purée into champagne glasses or glasses of a similar type and cover with coffee cream.

Coffee Cream

600ml (1 pint) milk
1 teaspoon cornflour
150ml (1/4 pint) strong black
  coffee
2 egg yolks

2 egg whites
100g (4oz) sugar
Vanilla essence
Grated chocolate

Take a little of the milk and mix it with the cornflour to a thin paste. Strain the coffee through a cloth and mix with the remaining milk.

Bring the coffee and milk mixture to the boil, add the cornflour and cook slowly for 5 minutes, stirring all the while. Remove from the heat and leave to cool. Beat the yolks with the sugar until they are frothy and add them to the coffee cream. Beat well for 1 to 2 minutes, then reheat and cook over a double boiler until the coffee mixture thickens. Add the essence, leave to cool again, and fold in the egg whites, previously stiffly beaten. Pour this cream over the chestnuts, and sprinkle with a little grated chocolate. Serve cold.

Italian cooking

'White Mountain'

Montebianco

This happens to be one of my favourite desserts, probably because I like almost anything cooked with chestnuts, which are not appreciated in England as much as I feel they should be. The Italians have a custom of offering a bowl of hot chestnuts and a bottle of wine as an impromptu meal for the unexpected guest. They also have a charming chestnut proverb, 'The chestnut is for the man who takes its shell off'.

450g (1lb) chestnuts
225ml (8fl oz) thick
 whipping cream

Vanilla essence
Milk
100g (4oz) caster sugar

Roast or boil the chestnuts until you are able to remove the outer shell and the inner skin. Return them to the pan, just cover with milk, add the sugar, and cook until they are soft enough to pass through a potato ricer or coarse wire sieve. The chestnuts should look like vermicelli after this process. Pile them into a cone shape, and then put them into the refrigerator or keep in a very cold place for several hours. Whip the cream until it is light, and just before serving the chestnuts completely cover the cone with the cream, so that the finished result is indeed a 'White Mountain'.

Usually I mix 1 stiffly beaten egg white in my cream simply to make it lighter.

Some cooks add grated chocolate to the chestnuts while they are cooking, and sprinkle the cone with it just before adding the cream. It is a matter of taste. For the amounts given above, 100g (4oz) of chocolate would be sufficient.

Stuffed Fresh Peaches

Pesche Ripiene

6 large ripe peaches
75g (3oz) sweet almonds
25g (1oz) toasted almonds
8 small macaroons

75g (3oz) sieved icing sugar
Brandy
1 tablespoon candied peel,
*   finely chopped*

This is a traditional sweet from Milan.

Scald the peaches for a moment or two in boiling water then peel off their skins. Halve lengthways, remove the stones, and scoop out a little of the pulp from each.

Grind the almonds finely. Mix with the sugar, the macaroons, previously crushed to fine crumbs, the peel and the peach pulp. Moisten with brandy, and when the mixture is well-blended put some into each of the peach halves. Rejoin the halves and fix with cocktail sticks. Brush with brandy and dust lightly with sieved icing sugar. Bake at 190°C/375°F/Gas 5 for about 20 minutes. They are nicest when heated brandy is poured over them and then set alight, but if you serve them cold with whipped cream they will still make a dish to remember.

Italian cooking

Orange Balls

Pallottole D'Arancia

Peel 6 large, thick-skinned oranges and 1 lemon. Remove all pith and soak the peel in cold water for 24 hours. Add 1 teaspoon of salt. Drain and wash thoroughly. Weigh the peel and then put it into a saucepan of cold water and bring slowly to the boil. Change the water and bring once more to the boil, then simmer until the peel is soft.

When the peel is tender drain and cut it very finely. Mix with its own weight in sugar, 25g (1oz) of which should be vanilla sugar.

Return to the saucepan and cook very slowly over a low heat for about 15 minutes or until a small amount dropped from a spoon into cold water forms a ball.

Leave the mixture to cool, then form it into balls and roll them first in icing sugar, then in finely ground hazel nuts.

Serve cold. They are rather good as an after dinner sweet.

If you prefer a more bitter-sweet taste, add more lemon peel and less orange peel.

Stuffed Oranges

Arance Ripiene

There are two ways of stuffing oranges:
1. Slice off the top of as many oranges as required, and carefully take out the pulp from each. Cut this into cubes, and mix it with an equal amount of fresh or frozen strawberries. Put the fruit into a bowl and flavour with brandy or kirsch to taste Sprinkle with caster sugar and leave for several hours in a cold place. Just before you are ready to serve the oranges pack them with the fruit, and cover with whipped cream.
2. Proceed as above, but only half fill the oranges with the mixed fruit. Add enough very firmly frozen ice-cream to almost reach the top of the orange and then cover this with meringue, making quite sure that the ice-cream is well insulated. Put the oranges into a very hot oven (240°C/475°F/Gas 9) for 1 minute and serve at once.

Egg Punch

Zabaglione

Zabaglione is probably one of the best known Italian sweets. It is served in glasses, either hot or cold, and is eaten with a spoon. For each egg used you need 1 tablespoon of sugar and 2 of Marsala. Whisk the eggs until they are a very pale lemon colour. Add the sugar and Marsala and whisk again until they are all well-blended. Put the mixture in the top of a double boiler and cook over boiling water until it thickens. Stir constantly while cooking and do not on any account let the mixture boil.

Coating Batter

100g (4oz) plain flour
1 beaten egg
150ml (1/4 pint) milk

Pinch salt
1 teaspoon baking powder
Sugar to taste

Sieve the baking powder with the flour. Add salt, sugar and then the egg. Beat until smooth, then gradually add the milk. Add more flour if too thin for coating, more milk if too thick.

Italian cooking

Sauces
Le Salse

Béchamel Sauce

La Besciamella

Recipes for this sauce vary from country to country. As far as the Italians are concerned it should be a basic white sauce. This is their recipe.

50g (2oz) butter
50g (2oz) sieved plain flour
300ml (1/2 pint) milk

Salt and pepper
Pinch nutmeg

Melt the butter and blend in the flour. Gradually add the milk, stirring all the time. Reduce the heat, add seasonings and nutmeg, and cook for 5 minutes.

Bolognese Sauce

Salsa Bolognese

50g (2oz) tomato purée
100g (4oz) raw beef or bacon, minced
75g (3oz) mushrooms, chopped
1 onion, chopped
1 tablespoon fresh parsley, chopped

1 teaspoon sugar
Salt and pepper
150ml (1/4 pint) dry white wine
600ml (1 pint) stock
Butter and olive oil

Heat 1 tablespoon of olive oil and 25g (1oz) of butter. Brown the parsley and onion, then add the mushrooms and the beef or bacon. Simmer for 3 minutes, add the wine, and continue to simmer the mixture until the wine has evaporated. Dilute the tomato purée with the stock, add the sugar, salt and pepper and pour this over the meat. Stir everything together well, continue to simmer for another 30 minutes.

Italian cooking

Green Sauce

Salsa Verde

Crush 2 cloves of garlic to a paste and add a heaped teaspoon of finely chopped fresh parsley, a tablespoon of capers, 3 anchovies and 1 small, chopped gherkin. Work together until a smooth paste is achieved. Add a very little grated onion, or, better still, onion juice, and 1 tablespoon of soft white breadcrumbs. Pour in a teaspoon of olive oil, drop by drop, then dilute with lemon juice until the mixture is fairly liquid.

A more simple version of the same sauce is to combine some finely chopped fresh parsley, capers and anchovies with 1 chopped hard-boiled egg. Add a vinegar and oil dressing and enough soft breadcrumbs to give body to the sauce.

Italian Dressing

Salsa

1 clove garlic	Fresh tarragon or mint
1 teaspoon French mustard	Lemon juice
Salt, pepper and sugar	Olive oil

Crush the garlic until smooth. Add the mustard, salt, pepper and sugar. Stir until smooth then add, drop by drop, a little lemon juice. When this is well-blended gradually work in about 2 tablespoons of good quality olive oil and just a touch of chopped, fresh tarragon or mint.

Italian Sauce

Salsa all'Italiana

1 heaped tablespoon of chopped
  fresh parsley
15g (1/2oz) dried mushrooms
50g (2oz) butter
1 teaspoon tomato purée

Salt and pepper
6 chopped shallots
125ml (4fl oz) vegetable stock
150ml (1/4 pint) sweet white wine
Juice 1/2 a lemon

For an authentic flavour use Italian mushrooms and soak for 30 minutes in tepid water. Chop them finely and sauté them with the parsley in butter, stirring all the time. As they begin to change colour add the shallots, salt and pepper and then the wine. Simmer until the wine is reduced to half, then add the tomato purée previously mixed with the stock and simmer for another 5 minutes. Add the lemon juice and serve hot with meat.

Lobster Sauce for Spaghetti

Salsa D'Arogosta

1 cooked lobster, or its tinned
  equivalent
1 large onion, chopped
600ml (1 pint) lobster stock
4 tomatoes, peeled and chopped

3 tablespoons olive oil
Fresh parsley and basil, chopped
2 cloves of garlic
25g (1oz) tomato purée
Salt and pepper

Heat the oil and fry the garlic, onion and parsley until brown. Add the tomatoes, salt, pepper and basil. Simmer for several minutes, add the stock and cook for 1 hour, or until the tomatoes are soft. Add lobster meat and continue simmering for 15 minutes.

If you are using tinned lobster then strain off all the liquid in the pan and use this with boiling water to make up to 600ml (1 pint).

Italian cooking

Butter Sauce

Salsa di Burro

Chop half an onion and a sprig of parsley very finely. Put both in a pan with 150ml (¼ pint) of a light white wine. Simmer until the amount of wine is reduced to a third. Cream 50g (2oz) of butter and gradually add it to the onion and parsley. Stir to a creamy, light and smooth consistency. On no account allow the butter to brown. Season with salt and pepper.

It is best to cook this sauce over boiling water.

Anchovy Sauce

Salsa d'Acciughe

Make a sauce with plain flour, butter and fish stock. Add a little chopped green pepper, fresh chopped parsley, crushed garlic, a few chopped capers and ground black pepper. Mash 8 anchovy fillets until soft and stir into the sauce. Stir until the sauce is well-cooked and smooth. Serve with hot fish.

Garlic and Anchovy Sauce

'Bagna Cauda'

This sauce is one of the specialities of Piedmontese cooking.

Melt 100g (4oz) of butter in an earthenware saucepan and very slightly brown 4 finely chopped cloves of garlic. Add 8 anchovies and stir these ingredients together with a wooden spoon. Serve very hot.

In Piedmont, truffles, which are plentiful, are added to the sauce.

It is usual to serve bagna cauda in the saucepan in which it is cooked and to serve it hot at the table. Pieces of uncooked vegetables, such as globe artichokes (a favourite continental vegetable), crisp celery or chicory are dipped in it.

Garlic Sauce

Aioli

Crush 4 cloves of garlic and a pinch of salt and work to a paste. Beat 1 yolk of an egg until it is absolutely smooth and gradually add it to the garlic. Add a teaspoon of olive oil, drop by drop as for mayonnaise, until you have a thick cream. Then gradually dilute this with lemon juice, using the whole of a lemon.

Lemon Sauce

Salsa al Limone

Make a white roux with 25g (1oz) of butter and 25g (1oz) of flour. Add enough warm milk to make a smooth white sauce. Season and cook fairly quickly for 10 minutes. Remove from the heat, allow the sauce to cool slightly, then whip in 2 well-beaten eggs. Return the sauce to the heat and gently reheat it. Add a tablespoon of chopped fresh parsley, a tablespoon of chopped capers and the juice of a large, juicy lemon. Stir until all the ingredients are well-blended.

This sauce can be eaten both with hot and cold meats.

Genoa Paste

Pasto alla Genovese

Crush 3 cloves of garlic, add plenty of fresh basil, 75g (3oz) of grated Pecorina cheese and a tablespoon of pine nuts and blend to a fine paste. Add olive oil, drop by drop, and thin the paste to a cream.

Another pesto is made from anchovies, garlic, fresh basil and cheese diluted with olive oil.

Pesto is usually served as a sauce with pasta or stirred into soup.

Italian cooking

Dried Mushroom Sauce

Salsa di Funghi

Use about 2 tablespoons of dried Italian mushrooms. Chop them fairly finely and soak them for 30 minutes in tepid water. Heat some butter in a pan, then lightly fry 1 finely chopped onion and a finely sliced stick of celery. Stir in 2 tablespoons of soft breadcrumbs and when all these ingredients are browned, add the mushrooms, stirring well. Add 1 tablespoon of tomato purée and enough vegetable stock to make a sauce, and simmer for 30 minutes. Season with salt and pepper then serve hot with either noodles or spaghetti.

Paprika Sauce

Salsa alla Paprika

Heat about 25g (1oz) of butter in a pan and lightly fry 1 to 2 finely chopped spring onions. Sprinkle in 25g (1oz) of plain flour, enough water to make a paste and stir, adding 1 tablespoon of paprika, the sweet Hungarian type, salt and pepper. Still stirring, gradually add enough milk to make a sauce of a béchamel consistency. About 1 to 2 tablespoons of cream beaten into the sauce is naturally a great improvement.

This sauce is good with goulash, thick stews, risottos, ragouts or savoury dishes.

Prune Sauce

Salsa di Prugne

Fry a chopped onion and 2 chopped rashers of bacon lightly in butter. Add 150ml (1/4 pint) of dry white wine and simmer until this has been reduced to half. Add about 100g (4oz) of prunes, previously soaked and stoned, salt, fresh thyme, sugar, 1 to 2 bay leaves and cold water to cover. Cook slowly until the prunes are soft, then rub everything through a sieve. Beat until smooth, dilute with a little more wine, then gently reheat.

Salad Dressing

Salsa Milano

Combine 4 tablespoons of olive oil with 2 tablespoons of red wine. Add a very little fresh basil, very finely chopped, a good pinch of English mustard powder and a level teaspoon of good quality anchovy paste. You will not need salt as the anchovy paste supplies enough.

Sauce for Osso Buco

Salsa per Osso Buco

Take some of the liquid from your Osso Buco (page 111), and put it into a small pan. Add a good handful of chopped fresh parsley, a chopped clove of garlic, some chopped lemon rind and chopped fresh rosemary and sage. Season with salt and pepper. Thicken slightly with a flour and water paste and simmer gently for 10 minutes. Serve hot.

Sauce Piquante

Salsa Piccante

Blend 225ml (8fl oz) of red wine with 225ml (8fl oz) of olive oil and 90ml (3fl oz) of wine vinegar. Add 1 finely chopped onion, 2 chopped cloves of garlic, half a teaspoon of dried red pepper seeds, a pinch of chopped fresh rosemary and salt. Whip well together so that they are perfectly blended, then leave them in a sealed jar for 24 hours.

This can be used either as a cold dressing for meats and fowl or as a basting mixture.

Italian cooking

Sweet-Sour Sauce

Salsa Agrodolce

50g (2oz) sugar
1 clove garlic
2 bay leaves

125ml (4fl oz) wine vinegar
50g (2oz) grated chocolate
Chicken stock

Cook the sugar in a thick saucepan until it is a light caramel colour. Add garlic, bay leaves, vinegar and chocolate. Simmer and stir until the chocolate melts, then add enough chicken stock to make a sauce of pouring consistency.

To be strictly authentic, you should use a gravy from venison or hare for this sauce.

Sweet-Sour Sauce for Fish

Salsa Agrodolce per Lessi

Heat 1 tablespoon of oil and 25g (1oz) of butter. Fry until brown a handful of chopped fresh parsley, a little chopped fresh basil and a small chopped onion. Add salt, pepper, a good pinch of cinnamon and 6 chopped tomatoes. Stir, then add 150ml (1/4 pint) of dry white wine and a heaped teaspoon of sugar. Simmer until the tomatoes are soft.

Tomato Sauce

Salsa di Pomidori

Sauce 1

Peel and slice 450g (1lb) of tomatoes into a saucepan with a chopped onion, carrot, celery, fresh thyme, fresh parsley and fresh basil or marjoram. Cook very gently for an hour. Rub through a sieve and season to taste. This is the simplest form of tomato sauce.

Sauce 2

Lightly brown 50g (2oz) of chopped bacon, or ham, in a mixture of olive oil and butter. Add 1 finely chopped onion, chopped fresh parsley and thyme, 1 to 2 bay leaves and fry until the onion is brown. Add a little plain flour, stir and cook until this too is brown, but take care not to burn it, then add 900g (2lb) of chopped tomatoes. Stir well and cook very gently for an hour, then rub through a sieve.

The Italians use prosciutto, and garlic may be added according to taste.

Tomato Sauce Piquante

Salsa alla Pizzaiola

Chop 2 cloves of garlic and brown them in olive oil. Add 4 peeled and chopped tomatoes and cook them quickly. Add a good measure of chopped fresh parsley and sweet marjoram and cook until the tomatoes are cooked through and can be rubbed through a sieve. Season with salt and pepper.

Truffle Sauce

Salsa di Tartufi

Although the cost of making this sauce in Britain would be prohibitive, it should be on record.

Heat 50g (2oz) of butter rather slowly and lightly brown 1 grated onion and 1 clove of garlic. Stir in 25g (1oz) of plain flour and pour in 90ml (3fl oz) of Marsala. Continue simmering and stirring until the sauce is smooth. Season with salt and pepper, remove the garlic and add a small slivered white truffle. Continue simmering over the lowest possible heat for 15 minutes. To be served with roast meats.

Italian cooking

Vegetarian Sauce for Spaghetti

Spaghetti di Magro

Fry very lightly in olive oil a chopped onion, carrot, turnip, parsnip, stick of celery, 2 tomatoes and 2 tablespoons of chopped fresh parsley. Season with salt and black pepper and add 600ml (1 pint) of hot vegetable stock. Simmer for 30 minutes.

When serving this sauce with spaghetti it is not usual to include grated cheese.

Sauces
Le Salse

Italian cooking

Italian cooking

Italian cooking

Index

Italian cooking

Notes

Notes

Notes

Notes

Notes

Notes

Notes

Notes

Notes

Notes

Notes

Notes

Notes

Notes

Notes

Notes